D0641483

Best Easy Day Hikes Series

Best Easy Day Hikes Death Valley National Park

Third Edition

Bill and Polly Cunningham WITHDRAWN

FALCONGUIDES

GUILFORD, CONNECTICUT
HELENA, MONTANA

To the thousands of citizens of California and elsewhere, past and present, who laid the groundwork for protection of much of the California desert, to those who helped secure passage of the landmark California Desert Protection Act, and to the dedicated park rangers and naturalists charged with stewardship of the national treasure that is Death Valley National Park.

FALCONGUIDES®

An imprint of Rowman & Littlefield
Falcon, FalconGuides, and Make Adventure Your Story are registered trademarks of Rowman & Littlefield.

Distributed by NATIONAL BOOK NETWORK

Copyright © 2000, 2011, and 2016 by Rowman & Littlefield

Maps DesignMaps Inc. © Rowman & Littlefield

All rights reserved. No part of this book may be reproduced in any form or by any electronic or mechanical means, including information storage and retrieval systems, without written permission from the publisher, except by a reviewer who may quote passages in a review.

British Library Cataloguing-in-Publication Information Available

Library of Congress Cataloging-in-Publication Data Available

ISBN 978-1-4930-1652-5 (paperback)
ISBN 978-1-4930-2726-2 (e-book)

♾™ The paper used in this publication meets the minimum requirements of American National Standard for Information Sciences—Permanence of Paper for Printed Library Materials, ANSI/NISO Z39.48-1992.

The authors and Rowman & Littlefield assume no liability for accidents happening to, or injuries sustained by, readers who engage in the activities described in this book.

Contents

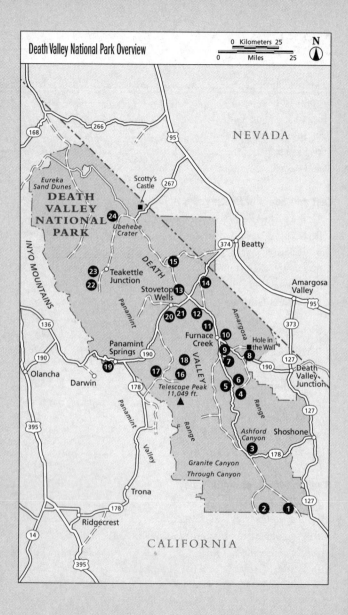

Acknowledgments

This book could not have been written without the generous assistance from knowledgeable park staff. Special thanks to Charlie Callagan, wilderness coordinator for the park and the leading authority on wilderness hiking in Death Valley. Charlie is a virtual fountain of information and enthusiasm for the park. He provided an in-depth review of our draft material time and again until he was satisfied that we finally had it right. We are especially grateful to Charlie for suggesting Room Canyon. Charlie was among the first to explore and document this wonderful place. We couldn't have done it without you, Charlie!

During our most recent winter visit to Death Valley, we based out of the Stovepipe Wells campground and had the pleasure of meeting camp host Phil Bender. Phil strives to help everyone enjoy the best camping experience possible and is truly the host with the most. Thanks, Phil!

And thanks to all the hospitable folks who provided advice and insights during our treks in the desert. Please know that you are not forgotten.

Thanks to you all!

Introduction

Death Valley National Park contains some of the planet's most imposing and contrasting landscapes—from North America's hottest, driest, and lowest desert to soaring snow-capped peaks. With such extremes Death Valley commands respect and entices discovery.

The California Desert Protection Act of 1994 upgraded and expanded the 2-million-acre Death Valley National Monument into today's 3.4-million-acre national park, 91 percent of which is designated and managed as wilderness under the landmark 1964 Wilderness Act.

Despite its ominous name, Death Valley hosts more than 400 year-round and seasonal wildlife species. More than 300 of these species are birds, the great majority of which are seasonal migrants. Most wildlife is nocturnal and usually unseen by the human eye. Your day hikes in the park will reveal spectacular desert scenery, complex geology, primeval wilderness, historical and cultural sites, and perhaps even a fleeting glimpse of rare wildlife.

This compact guidebook features easily accessible hikes that appeal to the full spectrum of visitors—from kids to grandparents. These twenty-four hikes sample the best that Death Valley has to offer, for the casual hiker and also for those in search of a mellow start to a longer, more difficult hike.

Most of the hikes in *Best Easy Day Hikes Death Valley* are short—less than 4 miles round-trip and with less than 600 feet of elevation change. More than half the hikes are ideal for families with small children. All of the trailheads can be reached with a passenger car, and about one-third are accessed by a paved road. The best easy day hikes are well distributed throughout the more accessible central portion of the sprawling park, which is served by paved highways going north to south and east to west.

For the most part, options listed at the end of some hike descriptions are extensions or longer variations of the hike. Consider these if you find yourself with that wonderful combination of additional time, energy, and determination.

Please keep in mind that the park has very few developed trails. The routes to Wildrose Peak and Telescope Peak are the only backcountry trails maintained by the park. Most hiking is up canyons, across salt flats and alluvial fans, or over dunes where any trail would soon be erased by ever-shifting sands. Fortunately, hiking on these natural trails is often easier than on constructed paths.

There is a park entrance fee per vehicle valid for seven days. The interagency America the Beautiful and Senior Access passes are honored as well. See the DVNP website for details.

For current information on park regulations, weather, campgrounds, park resources, hiking trails, and road conditions, contact Death Valley National Park at (760) 786-3200 or visit the park website. You can check the official park website for weekly ranger programs, including ranger-guided tours offered during the peak season of November through April. The Furnace Creek Visitor Center is open daily from 8 a.m. to 5 p.m. Before you begin hiking, be sure to stop at the visitor center to get updated regulations and other information that will make your trip more enjoyable.

Death Valley is busiest from February through mid-April, and in November. Surprisingly, the lowest visitation occurs during December and January, not during the hot summer months as you might expect.

Wildflowers

Rain throughout winter and spring, along with warm, sunny days and lack of drying winds, produces good wildflower years.

The park hosts more than 1,000 plant species, including twenty-three species endemic to the region as well as thirteen species of cactus. Desert annuals, like poppies and primroses, are the showiest.

Typical peak blooming periods are:

- Mid-February to mid-April at lower elevations (the valley floor and alluvial fans).
- Early April to early May for elevations between 3,000 and 5,000 feet (upper desert slopes, canyons, and higher valleys).
- Early May to mid-July for elevations above 5,000 feet (mountain slopes and pinyon pine/juniper woodlands).

Photography

The land of extremes that is Death Valley is best dramatized for the photographer when 11,049-foot Telescope Peak casts its afternoon shadow across the 282-feet-below-sea-level Badwater Basin. Combine this astounding vertical relief with recent volcanic craters, towering sand dunes, and flood-scoured canyons, and you'll see why knowledgeable photographers bring extra storage cards and batteries. These geologic wonders are most spectacular during the low-angle-light hours of morning and evening. Sunrises and sunsets are awe-inspiring.

Play It Safe

Wandering in the desert has a reputation of being a dangerous activity, thanks to both the Bible and Hollywood. Usually depicted as a wasteland, the desert evokes fear. With proper planning, however, desert hiking can be fun, exciting, and quite safe.

An enjoyable desert outing requires preparation. Beginning with this book, you need to be equipped with adequate knowledge about your hiking area. The potential hazards of desert hiking can be mitigated if you are prepared.

Dehydration

Plenty of water is necessary for desert hiking. Carry one gallon per person per day in unbreakable plastic screw-top containers, and pause often to drink it. Always carry water, even on short, easy hikes. As a general rule, plain water is a better thirst-quencher than any of the colored fluids on the market, which often generate greater thirst. Keep a gallon of water in your car so you have some available at the end of your outing, too.

Weather

Recorded temperatures range from a sizzling 134 degrees to a freezing low of 15 degrees. Summer temperatures average well above 100 degrees. In general, temperatures will be 3 to 5 degrees cooler, along with increased precipitation, for every 1,000-foot increase in elevation. For hiking comfort the months of November to April are hard to beat. Average highs are in the 60- to 90-degree range on the valley floor, cooling considerably at higher elevations. The higher peaks and ridges are often covered in snow from November to May.

An annual average of less than 2 inches of rain falls in the valley. During some years no rainfall is recorded. Ironically, flash floods are a persistent factor in sculpting the canyons and endangering hikers. See "Flash Floods."

The desert is well known for sudden changes in the weather. The temperature can change 50 degrees in less than an hour. Prepare yourself with extra food and clothing, rain and wind gear, and a flashlight.

Hypothermia/Hyperthermia

Abrupt chilling is as much a danger in the desert as heat stroke. Storms and/or nightfall can cause desert temperatures to plunge. Wear layers of clothes, adding or subtracting depending on conditions, to avoid overheating or chilling. At the other extreme, you need to protect yourself from sun and wind with proper clothing. A broad-brimmed hat is mandatory equipment for the desert traveler. Even in the cool days of winter, a delightful time in the desert, the sun's rays are intense. Don't forget the sunblock and lip sunscreen.

Vegetation

You'll quickly learn to avoid contact with certain desert plants. Catclaw, Spanish bayonet, and cacti are just a few of the botanical hazards. Carry tweezers to remove cactus spines and wear long pants if traveling in a brushy area.

Flash Floods

Desert washes and canyons can trap unwary visitors when rainstorms hit the desert. Keep a watchful eye on the sky. Check with the Furnace Creek Visitor Center (760-786-3200) for weather conditions before embarking on your backcountry expedition. A storm anywhere upstream in the drainage can cause a sudden torrent in a lower canyon. Do not cross a flooded wash. Both the depth and the current can be deceiving. Wait for the flood to recede, which usually does not take long, before crossing.

Lightning

Be aware of lightning, especially during summer storms. Stay off ridges and peaks during storms. Shallow overhangs and gullies should also be avoided because electrical current often moves at ground level near a lightning strike.

Rattlesnakes, Scorpions, and Tarantulas

Unexpected human visitors easily terrify these desert "creepy crawlies," and they react predictably to being frightened. Do not sit or put your hands in dark places, especially during the warmer "snake season" months.

Mine Hazards

Death Valley National Park contains numerous deserted mines. All of them should be considered hazardous. Because of this *all* mine adits in the park are closed to public entry. Stay away from all mine entrances and shafts and from mine structures. Keep an eye on young or adventuresome members of your group.

Unstable Rocky Slopes

Desert canyons and mountainsides often consist of crumbly or fragmented rock. Use caution when climbing, but be aware that the downward journey is usually the more hazardous. Smooth rock faces such as those found in slickrock canyons are equally dangerous, especially when you've got sand on the soles of your boots. On those rare occasions when they are wet, these rocks are slicker than ice.

Zero Impact

The desert environment is fragile; damage lasts for decades—even centuries. Desert courtesy requires us to leave no evidence that we were ever there. This ethic means no graffiti or defoliation at one end of the spectrum, and no unnecessary footprints on delicate vegetation on the other. Desert vegetation grows very slowly. Its destruction leads to wind and water erosion and irreparable harm to the desert.

The Falcon Zero-Impact Principles:

- Leave with everything you brought with you.
- Leave no sign of your visit.
- Leave the landscape as you found it.

Avoid making new trails. If hiking cross-country, groups should follow one set of footprints. Try to make your route invisible.

Keep noise down. Desert wilderness means quiet and solitude, for animals and other human visitors.

Pack it in and pack it out. This ethic is truer in the desert than anywhere else. Desert winds spread debris, and desert air preserves it. Always carry a trash bag, both for your trash and for any that you encounter. If you must smoke, pick up your butts and bag them.

Remember, artifacts fifty years or older are protected by federal law and must not be disturbed.

Treat human waste properly. Bury waste 4 inches deep and at least 200 feet from water sources and trails. Pack out toilet paper and feminine hygiene products; they do not decompose in the arid desert. Do not burn toilet paper; many wildfires have been started this way.

Respect wildlife. Living in the desert is hard enough for the wildlife without being harassed by human intruders. Please remember, this is the only home these animals have. Be respectful and use binoculars for long-distance viewing. Do not molest the rare desert water sources by playing or bathing in them.

Beyond these guidelines, refer to park regulations for specific rules governing backcountry use. Enjoy the beauty and solitude of the desert, and leave it as you found it for others to enjoy.

How to Use This Guide

To provide a geographic reference, hikes 1 through 15 are numbered south to north and are located east of Death Valley, in the eastern region of the park. Hikes 16 through 24, from south to north, are west and north of Death Valley, in the western and northern section of the park. The hikes presented in this book are rated according to difficulty, from easy to moderate. The "Ranking the Hikes" page will help you choose suitable hikes for everyone in your party.

Since established trails are rare in DVNP, we refer to "user trails." A user trail is an obvious footpath created by visitors that is not maintained by the park or another agency.

How to Get There

Primary access to the park from the east is NV 160 out of Las Vegas connecting with the Belle Vista Road out of Pahrump, Nevada, to CA 127. CA 190 heads west into the park from CA 127 at Death Valley Junction. From the south access is via CA 127 from I-15 at Baker. CA 178 leads west into the park from CA 127 near Shoshone. On the west side CA 178 takes off from US 395 and enters the park by way of Panamint Valley. CA 190 takes off to the east from US 395 at Olancha, entering the park just west of Panamint Springs. The nearest airport is in Las Vegas, Nevada, which provides a real contrast for your backcountry adventure in the wilderness of Death Valley.

Maps

The National Park Service Visitors Map is an excellent resource, both for overview trip planning and natural/human history information. The map referred to as Trails Illustrated Death Valley National Park Map in the map section for each hike is the Death Valley National Park topographic map (1:160,000 scale), published by Trails Illustrated/National Geographic. It is an ideal overview map for trip planning and navigating the roads between trailheads. In general, the more detailed 7.5-minute USGS topographic maps (1:24,000 scale) listed for each hike are not needed for hikes of less than 2 miles unless you are venturing beyond the described route. Refer to the small-scale hike maps provided in this book, especially for shorter interpretive trails that are typically well signed.

Campgrounds

To reserve a campsite in the Furnace Creek Campground, call (877) 444-6777 or go to www.recreation.gov. The rest of Death Valley's campgrounds are first come, first served, and there is a fee for most of them. Check the current fee schedule on the park website.

Pets in the Park: Leave Home without Them

You can bring your pet to the park, but it isn't a good idea for you or your best friend. Pets must always be on a leash or confined in a vehicle. They may not be left unattended in a campground. You cannot hike with them on trails, cross-country, or anywhere else off an established road. You can walk with them on a leash on backcountry roads, but with the above limitations designed to protect park values, it is best to share other experiences, not Death Valley, with your pet.

Ranking the Hikes

The following list ranks the hikes in this book from easiest to most challenging. The ranking applies only to the primary hike described, not to any options that may be included.

Easiest to Most Challenging

Trail Finder

Hikes for Birding

Map Legend

===6===	US Highway
===92===	State Highway
≡≡≡	Local Road
======	Unpaved Road
■■■■■	Featured Trail
------	Trail
········	Cross-Country Route
—··—··—	State Line
～～	River/Creek
⬭	Body of Water
✖	Airport
⌣	Bridge
▲	Campground
⟨⊔⊔⊔	Cliff
▲	Mountain/Peak
🅿	Parking
🛆	Picnic Area
■	Point of Interest/Structure
⟶	Spring
○	Town
⓫	Trailhead
◈	Viewpoint/Overlook
⩘	Waterfall

East and South of Death Valley

1 Ibex Sand Dunes

These remote sand dunes in a spectacular wilderness setting rise more than 150 feet and are trapped against rugged hills in the extreme southeastern corner of the park. From a distance the dunes appear taller than they are, making them even more impressive. Both the drive and the approach are relatively easy. The dunes are a picturesque and worthy destination in and of themselves, with added bonuses of expansive views and interesting mining ruins. Their isolation, hidden from paved roads by stark desert mountains, is a key attribute. This all adds up to an enjoyable romp in a giant sandbox.

Distance: 3 miles out and back to the mine ruins; up to 5 miles round-trip with side hikes in the dunes

Hiking time: 2 to 4 hours, depending on how much time is spent wandering in the dunes

Elevation change: 240 feet gain/loss

Difficulty: Easy for an out-and-back to the mine ruins; moderate if climbing the dunes, due to steep, loose sand

Trail surface: Firm footing on a closed two-track leading to the mine ruins with soft sand in places

Best season: November to April

Fees and permits: National Park entrance fee (see DVNP website for details)

Maps: NPS Death Valley Visitors Map; Trails Illustrated Death Valley National Park Map; USGS 1:24,000 topo maps Old Ibex Pass-CA and Saddle Peak Hills-CA

Special considerations: On rare occasions a recent rainstorm may cause the Amargosa River to flood portions of the Saratoga Springs Road, rendering it impassable. Dune boarding is destructive and illegal under both park service and wilderness regulations. Drinking water is unavailable, so carry ample water when hiking. Strong winds may reduce visibility with blowing sand. Do not attempt this hike during the heat of the summer or anytime when temperatures exceed 100 degrees F.

Trailhead facilities: None, but there is ample parking alongside the road.

Finding the trailhead: From Baker leave I-15 and drive 29.7 miles north on CA 127 to the Saratoga Springs Road, which is marked by the Harry Wade Monument. Turn left (west) on the narrow sandy gravel road (two-wheel-drive, high-clearance vehicle recommended) and drive 5.3 miles to a dirt road signed Saratoga Springs 4.4 miles. Turn right (north) and drive 2.6 miles, passing the turnoff to Saratoga Springs. Continue straight on the main road for another 0.9 mile and park next to a large wooden sign that reads Wilderness Restoration—foot and horse traffic only, marking a vehicular closure of an old road leading to mining ruins east of the dunes.

If approaching from the Badwater Road, take the slow gravel Harry Wade Road 25.7 miles to the signed Saratoga Springs Road.

From Shoshone drive 28.2 miles south on CA 127 to the Saratoga Springs Road, marked by the Harry Wade Monument. Turn right (west) and follow the above directions. GPS: N35 41.699' / W116 23.602'

The Hike

From the parking area the dunes rise directly to the east about 1 mile away. You can head straight cross-country on level open terrain to the low point between the two distinct complexes of sand dunes. Or walk slightly to the left of the wooden sign to pick up the closed two-track that leads to the same gap between the dunes and from there another 0.5 mile to the interesting ruins of a 1950s talc mine. The latter choice is slightly longer. Both routes offer solid footing across a hard-packed desert floor dotted with creosote bushes.

The dunes stretch more than 2 miles on a north-south orientation on the sunset side of the rugged Saddle Peak Hills. At roughly 1,300 acres they are the smallest dunes by area in the park. Their entrapment against high mountains fulfills one of the three conditions for dunes, the others being sand, of which there is an endless supply from nearby washes and canyons, and wind—also endless, especially during spring.

Like all dunes they are ever shifting. At the time of our visit, we climbed what was then the highest dune in the southern complex. Topping out at above 500 feet elevation, we looked down at the talc mine ruins 150 feet below. There are several types of dunes based on their shape. From this vantage point it appeared that most of the Ibex Dunes are barchan (crescent-shaped) dunes with arms that extend downwind.

It wasn't easy to reach this point. A narrow ridge with overstepped sides leads to the summit of each dune. The sides are often too steep to negotiate, leaving only the knife ridge for hiking, which is composed of soft sand. The payoff includes sweeping vistas of Death Valley, desert ranges to infinity, and a great feeling of wild, open space.

While traversing the dunes, especially around the edges, be on the lookout for Mojave fringe-toed lizards. Perhaps they dine on black beetles, of which you'll see lots. You'll also see wind ripples in the sand that resemble ocean waves.

From the dune ridges you can easily drop down to the abandoned talc mill. Like a ghost it hugs the rocky interface between the hills and the east side of the dunes. The ruins include several very deep and dangerous adits dug into the hillside next to the wooden mill—give them a wide berth. Park regulations, as well as common sense, require that you

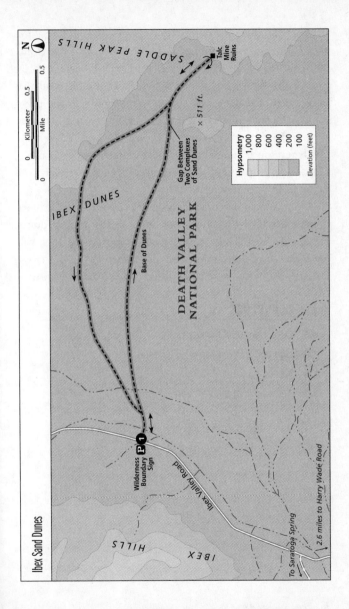

Ibex Sand Dunes

N

Hypsometry

Elevation (feet)
1,000
800
600
400
200
100

0   0.5
Kilometer

0   0.5
Mile

SADDLE PEAK HILLS

IBEX DUNES

Gap Between
Two Complexes
of Sand Dunes

× 511 ft.

Talc
Mine
Ruins

Base of Dunes

DEATH VALLEY
NATIONAL PARK

Wilderness
Boundary
Sign

P 1

Ibex Valley Road

IBEX HILLS

To Saratoga Spring

2.6 miles to Harry Wade Road

stay out of these hellacious holes. For more information about the history of mining in Death Valley, visit the Borax Museum (free admission) at Furnace Creek Ranch.

For the return you can follow the old mining road that leads north and then west for about 1.5 miles to the parking area. Notice how the dunes are reclaiming and gradually erasing the two-track where it crosses the gap between the north and south dunes. Nature will eventually prevail, but the old talc mill may stand for centuries given the slow rate of decay in the dry desert air.

If you want a longer sandy slog, hike up into the northern complex, which contains larger and slightly higher dunes. From there you'll see your vehicle alongside the Ibex Valley Road. From any point you can return by hiking cross-country 1-2 miles west to southwest to the parking area.

Miles and Directions

0.0 Depart from the trailhead.

1.0 Gap between north and south dunes.

1.5 Mine ruins.

3.0 Arrive back at the trailhead.

2 Saratoga Spring

A short stroll takes you to a desert oasis. Saratoga Spring is a spectacular surprise in the arid landscape of southern Death Valley. The spring is a mecca for fans of pupfish and many birds, including waterfowl, making it ideal for birdwatchers. There are also a couple of old stone building ruins for those interested in mining history.

Distance: 1.0-mile loop, or 0.8 mile out and back

Hiking time: About 1 to 2 hours, depending on how much you wander along the edge of ponds

Elevation change: Minimal

Difficulty: Easy

Trail surface: Old gravel two-track, sand

Best season: November to April

Fees and permits: National Park entrance fee (see DVNP website for details)

Maps: NPS Death Valley Visitors Map; Trails Illustrated Death Valley National Park Map; USGS 1:24,000 topo map Old Ibex Pass-CA

Special considerations: On rare occasions a recent rainstorm may cause the Amargosa River to flood portions of the Saratoga Springs Road, rendering it impassable. The road to the spring is signed for high-center vehicles, but with care a passenger car can make it. If wet, however, the sticky alkaline mud will make the final 1.3-mile track impassable.

Trailhead facilities: None, but there is a wide parking area at the end of the road. This is a day-use-only area; no camping is allowed.

Finding the trailhead: From Baker leave I-15 and drive 29.7 miles north on CA 127 to the Saratoga Springs Road, which is marked by the Harry Wade Monument. Turn left (west) on the narrow sandy gravel road (two-wheel-drive, high-clearance vehicle recommended but not required) and drive 5.3 miles to a dirt road signed Saratoga Springs 4.4 miles. Turn right (north) and drive 2.6 miles to the sign for Saratoga Springs. Turn left and drive 1.3 miles to the parking area. GPS: N35 40.840' / W116 25.261'

If approaching from the Badwater Road, take the slow gravel Harry Wade Road 25.7 miles south to the signed Saratoga Springs Road.

From Shoshone drive 28.2 miles south on CA 127 to the Saratoga Springs Road, which is marked by the Harry Wade Monument. Turn right (west) and follow the above directions.

The Hike

At the parking area a sign announces that the road is closed to vehicles. The old gravel two-track developed by miners many decades ago is our trail for the first third of the hike. At the top of the rise 0.1 mile northwest of the parking area, there is an awesome view of the spring, a series of ponds, surrounded by about 15 acres of lush grasses and reeds. The soft green landscape is quite a contrast with the rocky Ibex Hills. This desert wetland creates an inviting habitat for waterfowl and birds, as well as thirsty coyotes and desert bighorn sheep.

Continuing along the path, drop from the rise. The ruins of a small rock building are on the right. These walls are all that are left of what may have been a saloon, or perhaps a store dating from the 1890s development of the talc mine that left a white scar on the hillside to the north of the riparian area. There is a second, similar ruin farther along on the right. In the 1930s Saratoga Spring was briefly the site of a rustic health resort and a water bottling program. Both of these enterprises faded away with gas rationing during World War II.

At 0.2 mile the old roadbed continues north. Here, leave the track and drop toward the pond on your left. Exploring the water's edge is an adventure you don't expect in the desert. If you're stealthy, you can spot the shy Saratoga pupfish darting in the shallows. These tiny critters, *Cyprinodon nevadensis nevadensis*, are a different subspecies from the four other pupfish species elsewhere in the park region. In their isolated pools they are on the brink of extinction. This east side wetland relies on water from the ancient aquifer underlying the Black Range, which is an ever-diminishing resource. Please do not disturb the fish or their sensitive habitat. Stay out of the water.

The muddy shore of the ponds provides fascinating evidence of the many creatures who either visit or live here, leaving their footprints in the soggy, sandy soil. Instead of the usual silence of the desert, here the sounds of frogs and birds create a lively melody.

The small sandy dunes that surround the wetland create a natural route to travel around the ponds. A user trail takes you back to the main trail at the first overlook. This loop route is slightly longer than the out-and-back route.

Or, if you simply retrace your steps on your way back to the parking area, you might take a side trip to check out the mine adit, which you can see from the ponds, up behind the second ruin. Use caution, always, near mines. It was arduous work to dig a mine in these rocky hills. The slag heap that spills down the hillside is evidence of significant excavation. The miners didn't get rich here, but they sure had a lovely view.

After your explorations return to the parking area by the same route.

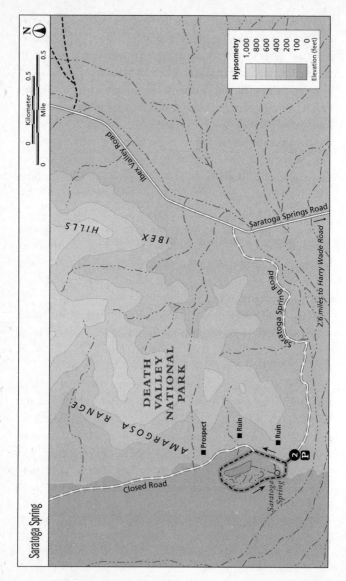

Saratoga Spring

Miles and Directions

0.0 Depart from the trailhead.

0.1 Top of the rise.

0.2 Leave roadbed.

0.4 Northern edge of pond complex (turnaround point for out and back).

1.0 Arrive back at the trailhead (loop route).

3 Room Canyon

Nothing about the view from the Badwater Road suggests the surprises that await you on this canyon hike. This is a unique slot canyon carved out of conglomerate, with boulders to crawl under and climb over. The elevation increase over the 2-mile hike to the turnaround is less than 300 feet, making it one of the flattest canyon hikes available in Death Valley.

Distance: 3.6 miles out and back

Hiking time: About 3 to 4 hours

Elevation change: 300 feet gain/loss

Difficulty: Easy

Trail surface: Cobbled wash, sandy wash

Best season: October to April

Fees and permits: National Park entrance fee (see DVNP website for details)

Maps: NPS Death Valley Visitors Map; Trails Illustrated Death Valley National Park Map; USGS 1:24,000 topo map Shore Line Butte-CA

Special considerations: Danger of flash flooding during heavy rains. Do not attempt this hike during the heat of the summer or anytime when temperatures exceed 100 degrees F.

Trailhead facilities: None, but there is ample parking along the Badwater Road.

Finding the trailhead: Drive 39 miles south of the Furnace Creek junction on the Badwater Road to milepost 39. Parking is available along the road. GPS: N35 58.571' / W116 43.631'

The Hike

From the parking area at the Badwater Road, the canyon mouth lies directly east. The low foothills below the towering peaks of the Black Range are deceiving. How can an exotic canyon be here? A wonderland awaits you.

Cast aside your doubts and head up the gentle alluvial fan toward the break in the low hills. Your pathway is the main wash coming down the alluvial fan, which provides a pretty clear walking surface. As you approach the hillsides, you may notice a patch of golden outcropping on the second row of hills on the right. Use the outcropping only as a marker. Room Canyon is to the north (left) of it.

Entering the opening between the foothills, about 0.7 mile from the road, bear north. The yellow conglomerate is replaced by red adobe on the pinnacles ahead. Just inside the canyon mouth, on the northwest wall, a flock of red pillars rises shakily above you. The group includes one remarkably skinny pillar, reaching like a finger to the sky. A user trail will take you up to the base of the pillars for closer inspection and for dramatic photographs. These are reputed to be the tallest free-standing pinnacles in the park!

As you continue into the canyon, surprises await at every bend. The canyon narrows to less than 10 feet wide almost immediately. Choke stones dangle overhead or create obstacles on the canyon floor. Children will enjoy the route, but overly large hikers will be challenged by the required crawl through a short tunnel. This is the most difficult maneuver on the hike.

At a junction about a mile from the road, a wide wash opens to the right. You can check it out on your way back, but your destination lies straight ahead. Like the winding streets of a medieval Moroccan village, the red walls lean over the narrow pathway. Huge tilted boulders leave a small space between the high canyon walls. At 1.3 miles from the trailhead lies the large oval Room, with majestic cathedral walls rising 300 feet or more on all sides. Just beyond the Room, a 25-foot stone obstruction blocks further exploration for most hikers since it requires a Class III scramble to bypass it. This is the turnaround for the casual hiker.

The Room is a fascinating spot, and perfect for dining. The silence of the canyon is broken by the twitter of the various birds whose nests ring the upper canyon walls. The power of erosion is visible everywhere, from the hoodoo spires to the drippy conglomerate stains frozen in rivulets on the canyon walls.

On your way out take a moment to explore the open wash to the left at the junction. The entry into the wash is immediately broad, almost panoramic after the close quarters of Room Canyon. A box canyon on the left (north), 0.2 mile up the wash, is blocked by a pour-off. Continue to the southeast, where the wash narrows to a canyon. Disorganized boulders litter the narrow canyon floor, creating challenges and obstacles, until you reach the final pour-off at 0.5 mile from the junction. These canyons are subject to constant remodeling.

Retrace your path to the trailhead, enjoying the cool of the canyon before you hit the valley floor.

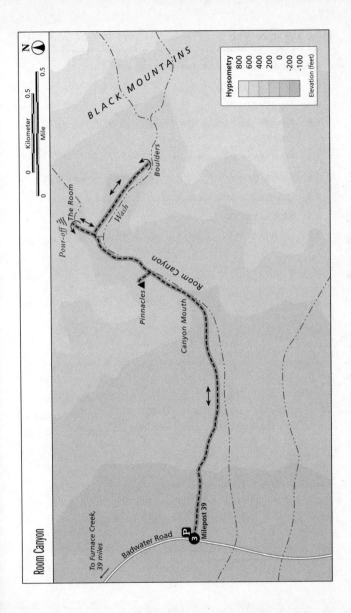

Room Canyon

BLACK MOUNTAINS

Boulders

Pour-off The Room

Wash

Pinnacles

Room Canyon

Canyon Mouth

To Furnace Creek,
39 miles

Badwater Road

P
3
Milepost 39

N

0   Kilometer   0.5
0   Mile   0.5

Hypsometry
800
600
400
200
0
-200
-100
Elevation (feet)

Miles and Directions

0.0 Depart from the Badwater Road trailhead.

0.7 Mouth of canyon.

0.8 Pinnacles.

1.0 Junction; wash to the right. Continue left up the narrow canyon.

1.3 The Room; turnaround point.

1.6 Back to the junction; turn into the open wash on the left.

2.1 End of open wash; turnaround point.

2.6 Back to junction.

3.6 Arrive back at the trailhead on the Badwater Road.

4 Dante's View and Peak

This short, easy hike offers magnificent panoramic views of the highest and lowest points in the continental United States. Surrounded by some of the most dramatic and colorful relief found anywhere, you are nearly 6,000 feet directly above the lowest spot in the nation at Badwater.

Distance: 1 mile out and back
Hiking time: Less than 1 hour
Elevation change: 229 feet
Difficulty: Easy
Trail surface: Clear trail
Best season: October through June
Fees and permits: National Park entrance fee (see DVNP website)
Maps: NPS Death Valley Visitors Map; Trails Illustrated Death Valley National Park Map; USGS 1:24,000 topo map Dante's View-CA
Trailhead facilities: There is a large signed parking area with interpretive signs at the end of the paved road. The road climbs gradually, passing by an interim parking area just before the final quarter mile, which has a grade of 14 percent.

Finding the trailhead: From CA 190, 11.9 miles southeast of the Furnace Creek Visitor Center and 18 miles west of Death Valley Junction, turn south on the signed Dante's View Road (paved, all-weather). Drive 13.3 miles on this steep, winding road to its end at the Dante's View parking area. GPS: N36 13.238' / W116 43.603'

The Hike

The unsigned trail to Dante's Peak is clearly visible to the north as it climbs toward Dante's Peak from the parking area. If possible, take this hike in the early morning with the sun at your back. This makes for better photography and for enhanced enjoyment of the superlative vistas and astounding 5,986-foot drop to the salt flats of Badwater, which sits 282 feet below sea level. The temperature at Dante's View averages 25 degrees cooler than that of Badwater. This exposed location is usually windy, necessitating a windbreak garment for the hike.

This lofty vantage point in the Black Mountains enables you to almost see, or at least visualize, how the mountains are both rising and slowly moving to the left (south) relative to the surrounding terrain. Looking across Death Valley to the highest point in the park, 11,049-foot Telescope Peak, you can easily note the major vegetative life zones stretching westward like a giant map. Bristlecone and limber pines thrive high in the Panamint Range. Below is the pinyon pine–juniper zone. Dante's View is situated in a hotter, drier midslope of blackbush and sage. Floods from the mountains result in graveled fans that support spreading root species such as creosote bush. Fresh water displaces salt from the fan edges, allowing mesquite to grow. Pickleweed gains a foothold in the brackish water below these edges. The muddy tans and grays of the valley floor grade into white beds of almost pure salt—a chemical desert.

From the parking lot hike north along the road for 0.1 mile to where the Dante's Peak trail begins a fairly steep climb up the hill. Soon it winds to the left (west) and contours gently along the mountain's west slope. This route provides an even more impressive view down to Badwater, with an almost overwhelming vertical relief dropping more than a mile straight down! At 0.3 mile, the trail intersects the summit ridge, then climbs the short distance to the 5,704-foot-high point. Although unofficial, the trail is clear, well defined, and easy to follow. Return the way you came to complete this 1-mile out-and-back ridge walk, and don't forget your camera.

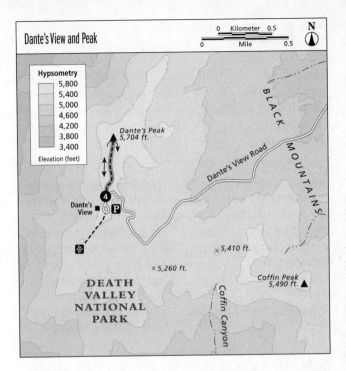

Dante's View and Peak

Hypsometry
- 5,800
- 5,400
- 5,000
- 4,600
- 4,200
- 3,800
- 3,400

Elevation (feet)

BLACK MOUNTAINS

Dante's Peak
5,704 ft.

Dante's View Road

Dante's View

P

4

× 5,410 ft.

× 5,260 ft.

DEATH
VALLEY
NATIONAL
PARK

Coffin Canyon

Coffin Peak
5,490 ft. ▲

Option

For a slightly different perspective, hike a well-used path 0.25 mile southwest of the parking area. The rock outcropping at the point of the ridge is especially useful as a windbreak for setting up a tripod for early morning photography.

Miles and Directions

0.0 Depart from the trailhead.

0.3 The trail intersects the summit ridge.

0.5 Reach Dante's Peak.

1.0 Arrive back at the trailhead.

5 Badwater

This is a perfectly flat hike on a boardwalk that leads you onto the salt flats at the hottest and lowest point in the United States and the lowest elevation you can drive to in the Western Hemisphere. This vast bed of salt lies 282 feet below sea level.

Distance: 1 mile out and back on boardwalk or 2 miles out and back into the salt flats
Hiking time: Less than 1 hour
Elevation change: Minimal
Difficulty: Easy
Trail surface: Boardwalk, clear salt flat
Best season: November through March

Fees and permits: National Park entrance fee (see DVNP website)
Maps: NPS Death Valley Visitors Map; Trails Illustrated Death Valley National Park Map; USGS 1:24,000 topo map Badwater-CA
Trailhead facilities: There is a signed parking area alongside a paved highway along with vault toilets and interpretive signs.

Finding the trailhead: The signed parking area for Badwater is on the west side of the Badwater Road, 16.7 miles south of the CA 190 junction at the Furnace Creek Inn. GPS: N36 13.823' / W116 46.273'

The Hike

As bleak as it looks, the popular hike onto the salt flats at Badwater is arguably the ultimate Death Valley experience. If you have been to Dante's View or Telescope Peak, you probably saw the human ants on the white expanse of valley floor and wondered what could be so fascinating. Here you will find individuals, especially families, cavorting like they're at the beach or enjoying a spring snow. To gain a genuine sense of the enormity of the salt flats, hike beyond the heavily traveled section.

The hike begins at the parking area beneath the cliffs that soar up to Dante's View, 5,542 feet above. There's a sea level sign on the cliff face, high above Badwater, making very clear what minus 280 feet represents. Walk out to the salt flats on the causeway, but continue beyond the well-trod area, depending on the temperature and wind, to a clear area of the flats. Getting away from the highway and the boardwalk is essential to get a sense of the magnitude of the salt flats. You'll reach the edge of the 5-mile-wide salt flats at minus 280 feet after only 0.5 mile. The actual lowest point in North America of minus 282 feet is another 3-mile hike across the salt flats to the northwest of Badwater.

Here, salt crystallizes when the groundwater that carries it to the earth's surface hastily evaporates. If you sit on the salt flats, you will find yourself among tiny salt pinnacles, a miniature mountainous world at the bottom of this mountainous basin. In close contact with the surface you will also discover that salt is a tough commodity. The white flooring of the flats is only inches thick, but very firm underfoot. Salt's power as an erosive force is noteworthy in this desert, where it functions much like frost heaves and ice do in a wet climate. Salt crystals grow and force apart boulders, breaking them down to be further eroded by wind and water. The salt crystal crust may be covered with a temporary lake following a rare heavy rainstorm.

Above the microworld of salt, the world of Death Valley soars. Less than 19 miles to the west is Telescope Peak

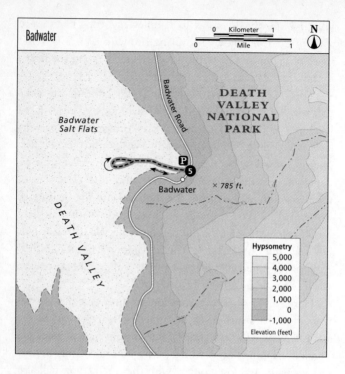

0   Kilometer   1

0   Mile   1

N

Badwater Road

DEATH VALLEY NATIONAL PARK

Badwater Salt Flats

Badwater   × 785 ft.

DEATH VALLEY

Hypsometry

Elevation
5,000
4,000
3,000
2,000
1,000
0
-1,000

Elevation (feet)

(11,049 feet), the park's highest point. The difference in elevation between Badwater and Telescope Peak is one of the largest in the United States.

A hike at Badwater is an essential introduction to the expanse of the valley floor. The emigrants and the miners who lived in this environment were a tough lot.

The glare from the salt flats can be as intense as on snowfields at high elevation. Wear sunglasses. Do not hike to the salt flats during the extreme heat of summer. Keep in mind that when the temperature tops 100 degrees F, ground temperatures exceed a sizzling 180 degrees F!

Miles and Directions

0.0 Depart from the trailhead.

0.5 Reach the end of the boardwalk at the edge of the salt flats. Return to the trailhead or continue hiking into the flats.

1.0 Turn around and retrace your steps toward the trailhead from the boardwalk hike.

2.0 Arrive back at the trailhead from the salt flats hike.

6 Natural Bridge

A gently sloped canyon leads to a natural bridge that arches over the canyon bottom. The geological phenomena—faults, slip faulting, chutes and dry falls, natural arch formations—are explained at a trailhead exhibit.

Distance: 2 miles out and back
Hiking time: 1 to 2 hours
Elevation change: 520 feet
Difficulty: Easy
Trail surface: Sandy canyon bottom
Best season: October through April
Fees and permits: National Park entrance fee (see DVNP website)

Maps: NPS Death Valley Visitors Map; Trails Illustrated Death Valley National Park Map; USGS 1:24,000 topo map Devil's Golf Course-CA
Trailhead facilities: There is a large signed parking area with vault toilets and interpretive signs at the end of the dirt road.

Finding the trailhead: From the intersection of CA 190 and the Badwater Road in Furnace Creek, drive south on the Badwater Road for 14.1 miles. Turn left (east) on the signed dirt road, and drive 1.5 miles to the Natural Bridge parking area. The road is washboardy and rough but is suitable for standard two-wheel-drive vehicles. The trail begins behind the information kiosk. GPS: N36 16.921' / W116 46.069'

The Hike

Death Valley's fascinating geologic history is featured on the informational kiosk at the trailhead of the Natural Bridge hike. Bedding and slip faulting are explained on the board, so the canyon's convoluted display is even more impressive.

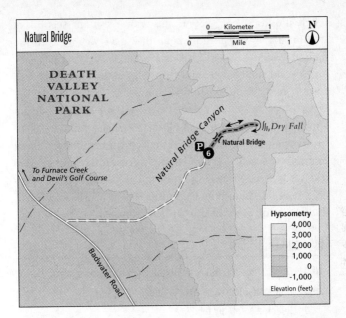

Likewise, differential erosion is described and illustrated, preparing you for the bridge. Fault caves, the metamorphic layers of the Artist's Drive Formation, and mud drips are other topics covered in this condensed, well-written version of physical geology.

The canyon floor consists of loose gravel; that and its sharp slope suggest a relatively young canyon. Death Valley's floor continues to subside while the Funeral Mountains rise. Dynamic geologic forces are still active here.

The trail begins by passing through deeply eroded volcanic ash and pumice canyon walls. The gravel wash maintains a steady 6-percent grade as the canyon gradually narrows. At 0.3 mile the high bridge arches over the canyon bottom. An ancient streambed is visible to the north of the bridge, where floods swept around this more resistant section of stratum before the pothole beneath it gave way to form the natural bridge.

Beyond the bridge, mud drips, slip faults, and fault caves appear, reinforcing the information you picked up at the kiosk. You can climb a dry fall at mile 0.8 with moderate effort, but a 20-foot dry fall blocks travel at 1 mile.

Retracing your steps down the canyon reveals even more examples of geology in action. Ever-shifting light creates iridescent colors. Traveling in the same direction as the powerful flash floods and the loads of scouring debris emphasizes the impact of water in this arid environment.

Miles and Directions

0.0 Depart from the trailhead northeast of the parking area.

0.3 A natural bridge arcs over the trail.

0.8 Reach a small dry fall.

1.0 The canyon is blocked by a 20-foot dry fall.

2.0 Arrive back at the trailhead.

7 Artist's Dips

Close to Furnace Creek and right off the busy Artist's Drive, this 4.5-mile outing takes you swiftly into dramatic solitude, with the vivid strata of colorful volcanic formations rising above the canyons. Review your crayon vocabulary before this hike so you can describe the colors!

Distance: 4.5-mile loop
Hiking time: 2 to 4 hours
Elevation change: 600 feet gain/loss
Difficulty: Moderate, with two modest dry falls (5 and 7 feet, respectively)
Trail surface: Desert wash, some cobbles, sand
Best season: October to April
Fees and permits: National Park Entrance Fee (see DVNP website)
Maps: NPS Death Valley Visitors Map; Trails Illustrated Death Valley National Park Map; USGS 1:24,000 topo map Devils Golf Course-CA
Special considerations: Flash flood danger in the washes. Do not attempt this hike if it has rained heavily, is raining heavily, or it might rain. Do not attempt this hike during the heat of the summer or anytime when temperatures exceed 100 degrees F.
Trailhead facilities: None, but there is a parking area along Artist's Drive.

Finding the Trailhead: From the junction below the Furnace Creek Inn, drive south on the Badwater Road 8.5 miles. Turn left on the one-way Artist's Drive (signed). There are two large dips on the road. The first one is at 2.9 miles. That dip is where the hike will start, but the best parking is along the road, 0.4 miles farther, at the top of the rise. The second dip (also signed) will be your exit, so you will walk back 0.1 mile to your car when you finish the hike. GPS: N36 21.131' / W116 47.609'

The Hike

From the rise between the dips, return southward 0.4 miles to the low point back at Dip 1. Turning your back on the lofty Artist's Palette, head west, down the wash. The wide mouth becomes narrow and loses elevation quickly, so the presence of the nearby road quickly disappears. Ironically, almost immediately you can spot evidence of an old roadbed on the south (left) canyon wall. Shortly you cross the remnants of the old pavement where the former road crossed the wash. This is a marvelous place to pause and observe the impact of pavement on accelerating erosion. Continue down the wash. Telescope Peak cuts the skyline straight to the west.

Your descent reveals a glorious array of geologic layers, from gravelly conglomerates to multicolored volcanic ash sediments to burnt umber lava flows. If it is a wet spring, there will be flowers galore. Tenacious desert holly lines the gravel bottom. Gravel ghost erupts where there's enough moisture from rivulets off the canyon walls. Patches of desert five-spot flourish in the sandy bottoms where water exists. Ubiquitous creosote thrives in the middle of the wash.

The dark canyon walls rise as you descend. What initially may have looked like a mundane wash has now become a dramatic canyon. Continue downward in the canyon. If any junction tempts you, check whether you can see the Badwater Valley floor ahead in the distance. If you don't see it, don't turn out of the main canyon. Not yet.

The gravel pathway continues to drop. It makes a sharp right turn (north) where fault lines are clearly visibly on the cliff face and the tilted layers are sharply angled. A stretch of narrows extends from 1.2 to 1.5 miles from the road.

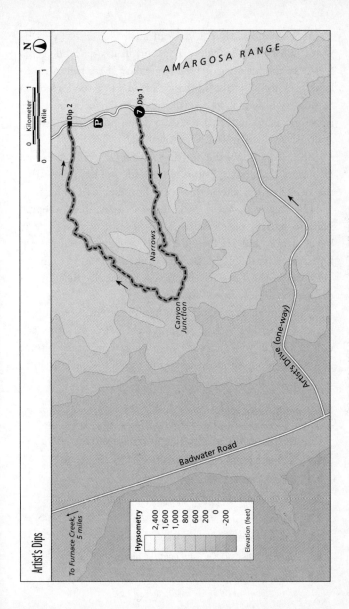

Artist's Dips

AMARGOSA RANGE

N

0 Kilometer 1
0 Mile 1

Dip 2

P

7 Dip 1

Narrows

Canyon
Junction

Artist's Drive (one-way)

Badwater Road

To Furnace Creek,
5 miles

Hypsometry

2,400
1,600
1,000
800
600
200
0
-200
Elevation (feet)

At 2 miles from Dip 1 you can finally see all of the Bad-water Valley floor far below. The canyon has descended 600 feet since the hike began. Here you take a sharp right turn to head back uphill in the adjacent canyon. Here too a plethora of flowers bloom in the spring if there has been adequate moisture. Ants are busy harvesting desert holly seeds, leaving a wreath of chaff around their mounds.

At 0.5 mile above the junction, a 5-foot dry fall is followed by a more challenging 7-foot one. Hand- and footholds make the ascents secure, although a boost from behind can help.

The soaring, fluted red canyon walls, the weeping Navaho red on the vertical pink walls, the walls of green, burnt sienna, and orange—the hike back up to the road at Dip 2 is a visual delight. Be sure to turn around to grab the view down the canyon behind you to get the full dose of dramatic colors, textures, and angles.

The canyon reverts to a wash and flattens as you draw nearer to Artist's Drive. Emerging right below Banish Canyon at Dip 2, you end your hike by turning right (south) and hiking along the road up to the top of the rise, 0.1 mile, where you left your car.

Miles and Directions

0.0 From the parking area head south along the road back to Dip 1.

0.4 Turn west (right) down the wash.

1.6 Canyon narrows.

2.4 Canyon junction. Turn sharp right (northeast).

2.9 Dry falls.

3.1 Canyon narrows.

4.4 Back at Artist's Drive. Turn right (south) to your vehicle.

4.5 Arrive at parking area.

8 The Mummy

This short hike has everything going for it in a compact package. Within only 1 mile you'll see a huge distinctive formation, a small arch, a natural bridge, and a glimpse of history thrown in for good measure. And to top it off, Mummy Canyon is easily accessible from a paved road.

Distance: 1.8 miles out and back
Hiking time: 1 to 2 hours
Elevation change: 440 feet gain/loss
Difficulty: Easy
Trail surface: Gravel outwash and sandy canyon bottom with some short rocky sections
Best season: October to May
Fees and permits: Park entrance fee (see DVNP website)
Maps: NPS Death Valley Visitors Map; Trails Illustrated Death Valley National Park Map; USGS 1:24,000 topo map Echo Canyon-CA
Special considerations: There is no designated parking area for this unsigned hike. It is important to parallel park next to the busy highway in a safe location. The park entrance sign is a popular photo op, so please avoid blocking the view by parking a good distance west of the sign, or just to the east of it.

Finding the trailhead: Park alongside CA 190 some 12.3 miles southeast of the CA 190/Badwater Road junction and about 0.2 mile west of the park boundary sign on the north side of the highway. Look for a wide, safe pullout with good visibility in both directions. The parking area is about 13 miles southeast of Furnace Creek. GPS: N36 22.556' / W116 41.328'

The Hike

From the parking area climb a low berm and drop into the main Furnace Creek Wash. Look down the wash and you'll see a side canyon that enters from the right, bound by brown columnar hillsides. This is Mummy Canyon. You can actually see the backside of the mummy-shaped formation from here, which blends into the hillside on the far side of the canyon. As you get a lot closer, you'll know it when you see it.

Walk down the cobblestone wash as it parallels the road about 0.2 mile to the wide mouth of Mummy Canyon, which is also known as Jensen Canyon. At the mouth veer right and head straight north toward the canyon. Notice the amazing array of cacti, with the most prominent being beavertail, barrel, prickly pear, and silver cholla. The right side of the lower canyon is overseen by a large sphinx-shaped rock next to a small arch. After about 0.4 mile more, the canyon begins to narrow dramatically. Striking vertical white streaks of travertine calcium carbonate deposits are embedded in steep slopes of brown conglomerate. Vertical canyon walls have weathered in a honeycomb pattern. Some of the larger chunks of conglomerate in the bottom contain beautiful inlaid pebbles and small rocks glued by quartzite and silica. You'll soon reach a perfect 30-foot-high half-circle alcove that marks the entrance to a second set of even tighter narrows. These narrows end all too quickly at an impassable dry fall under a small but very impressive natural bridge. You've reached the turnaround point.

If you stand directly underneath the bridge and look up, you'll have the sensation of gazing straight up into a tunnel. Over the eons floodwaters have poured over the dry fall and

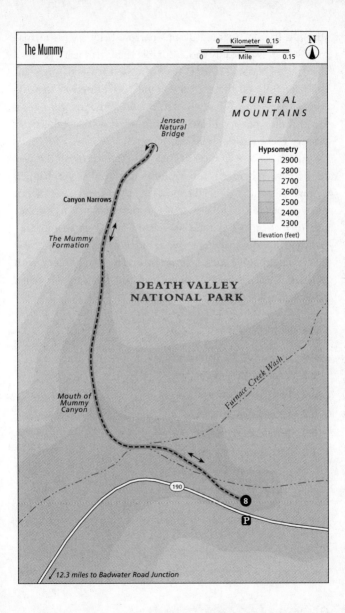

The Mummy

0　Kilometer　0.15
0　Mile　0.15

N

FUNERAL MOUNTAINS

Jensen Natural Bridge

Canyon Narrows

The Mummy Formation

DEATH VALLEY NATIONAL PARK

Furnace Creek Wash

Mouth of Mummy Canyon

Hypsometry

2900
2800
2700
2600
2500
2400
2300

Elevation (feet)

190

8

P

↙ 12.3 miles to Badwater Road Junction

through the slot formed by this narrow bridge. This formation, which is probably more durable than it appears, is called the Jensen Natural Bridge. If you missed it on the way up, look carefully on the way down and you'll discover the reason for the name. What you'll find is an authentic glimpse of Death Valley history. Leave it undisturbed so that others can ponder the question, who was Jensen?

Another point of interest that you might miss on the way to the natural bridge is the Mummy itself, unless you happen to turn around at the right spot. Otherwise you can't miss it during your return hike back down the canyon. This distinctive formation is a natural likeness of an Egyptian mummy, standing up, on the right (west) side of the canyon going down. The massive rock column towers nearly 200 feet, with detailed facial features looking back up the canyon. Huge arms are folded up toward the head.

Miles and Directions

0.0 Depart from the parking area.

0.2 Mouth of Mummy Canyon.

0.6 First canyon narrows.

0.8 Second canyon narrows.

0.9 Jensen Natural Bridge.

1.8 Arrive back at the parking area.

9 Desolation Canyon

Desolation Canyon is a highly scenic but less crowded alternative to the nearby Golden Canyon. This short hike features moderate canyoneering to a high pass overlooking the Artist's Drive Formation. The deep, narrow, colorful canyon provides a feeling of solitude, with broad vistas from the overlook.

Distance: 4.2 miles out and back

Hiking time: 2 to 3 hours

Elevation change: 750 feet gain/loss to overlook

Difficulty: Moderate

Trail surface: Clear wash with three short rock pitches

Fees and permits: National Park entrance fee (see DVNP website)

Best season: Early November to mid-April

Maps: NPS Death Valley Visitors Map; Trails Illustrated Death Valley national Park Map; USGS 1:24,000 topo map Furnace Creek-CA

Finding the trailhead: From the Death Valley Visitor Center in Furnace Creek, drive southeast 1.2 miles to the junction of CA 190 and the Badwater Road; turn right (south) onto the Badwater Road and drive 3.7 miles to the unsigned parking area, which is to the left along the east side of the highway. The old road was washed out by the big thunderstorm flood of August 2004. Drive 0.5 mile to the new parking area. The topographic map incorrectly identifies the immediate canyon to the south as Desolation Canyon. In fact, Desolation Canyon is the longer and wider canyon to the immediate southeast of the parking area. GPS: N36 23.728' / W116 50.345'

The Hike

This is an enjoyable and highly scenic canyon hike for anyone, but it is especially appreciated by those without a four-wheel-drive vehicle, in that access is just off the paved highway. Despite its proximity to both the Badwater Road and Artist's Drive, the narrow canyon provides a deep feeling of intimacy and solitude. The entire out-and-back trip offers a superb opportunity to observe the dynamics of badlands erosion, which is everywhere, from mud-filled gullies to bizarre eroded shapes overlooking the canyon.

Because Desolation Canyon involves a short hike at low elevation, the recommended time of day for the hike is mid- to late afternoon, when the cooler shadows fill the canyon. Upon return, late afternoon to early evening, brilliant light can be spectacular on the multicolored east-facing slopes above the canyon.

Begin the hike by following the old washed-out road from the far end of the parking loop. It wraps around the toe of Desolation's west ridge and then leads southeasterly into the broad lower wash of Desolation Canyon at 0.6 mile. At first the wide wash climbs gently, gradually increasing gradient to the first canyon junction. Stay to the right in the main canyon at several junctions that appear during the first mile. Soon the canyon narrows with even narrower side draws. Desolation isn't a true slot canyon, but in places its walls are close enough that you can touch both sides at once.

The next 0.1 mile brings a couple of stair-step rocks that are easy to climb, before the canyon again widens. At around 1.6 miles what appears to be the main canyon to the left ends at a dry waterfall another 0.1 mile up. Continuing up the narrower canyon to the right leads you to a steep, unstable

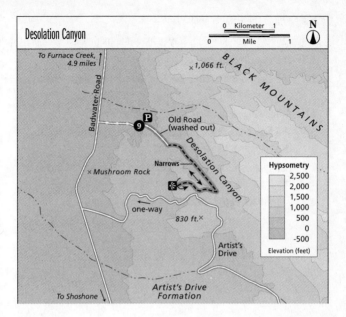

rock chute at 2 miles. This is a good turnaround point. Assuming you still have the urge and energy to explore, climb up to the right on loose, deep gravel to the 700-foot-elevation overlook at 2.1 miles. This relatively lofty vantage point provides a spectacular view of the varied colors of the Artist's Drive Formation to the south. From this point the Artist's Drive road is directly below about 0.3 mile. Return by way of Desolation Canyon to complete this colorful 4.2-mile round-trip badlands/canyon excursion.

Miles and Directions

- **0.0** Start at the trailhead/parking area.
- **0.6** At the intersection with the Desolation Canyon wash, turn right up the canyon.

0.8 Where the canyon splits, stay right.

0.9 At the canyon junction, stay right up the main wash.

1.1 The canyon steepens, requiring moderate scrambling.

1.2 The canyon widens to a junction. Go right up the steeper, less colorful canyon with more stair-step rocks.

1.6 At the canyon junction, stay right up a narrow gully.

2.0 The hike ends where the canyon reaches a steep chute. This is an optional turnaround point.

2.1 Scramble up a very steep, unstable slope westward (right) to the overlook.

4.2 Arrive back at the trailhead via the same route.

10 Golden Canyon/Gower Gulch Loop

This fascinating journey through geologic time passes by rocks of different ages as the elevation increases, then loops back down to the floor of Death Valley past borax mine tunnels. The first section is an educational geology nature trail. The scenery of the extended trip includes a colorful lakebed, exposed strata, and alluvial fan formations, along with spectacular scenery of the Panamint Range from below Zabriskie Point.

Distance: 2 miles out and back; 6.5 miles for complete optional loop with side trips
Hiking time: 1 to 2 hours for short hike; 3 to 5 hours for longer loop
Elevation change: 300 feet for short hike; 750 feet for complete loop
Difficulty: Easy (short hike); moderate (longer hike) due to distance and elevation gain
Trail surface: Sandy trail and rocky wash

Best season: November through April
Fees and permits: National Park entrance fee (see DVNP website)
Maps: NPS Death Valley Visitor Map; Trails Illustrated Death Valley National Park Map; USGS 1:24,000 topo map Furnace Creek-CA
Trailhead facilities: The signed trailhead and parking area, with vault toilet, bulletin board, and interpretive guide to the trail, are adjacent to the paved highway.

Finding the trailhead: From CA 190, 1.2 miles south of the Furnace Creek Visitor Center, head south on the paved Badwater Road. After 2 miles turn left (east) into the Golden Canyon parking area and trailhead, which is on the east side of the road. From the south, 2 miles north of the small town of Shoshone, turn west onto CA 178 and continue into the park. From Ashford Junction, go north on the

Badwater Road. The signed Golden Canyon parking area is 14.4 miles north of Badwater and can be seen just off the highway to the right (east). GPS: N36 25.246' / W116 50.795'

The Hike

Both the shorter and longer versions of this hike provide an incredible journey through geologic time, passing rocks of different ages as the elevation increases. An excellent interpretive trail guide to the Golden Canyon Trail is available for 50 cents at the Golden Canyon trailhead. Ten stops in this geology guide are keyed to numbered posts along the trail.

Golden Canyon was once accessed by paved road. In February 1976 a four-day storm caused 2.3 inches of rain to fall on nearby Furnace Creek—one of the driest places on earth (where no rain fell during all of 1929 and 1953). Runoff from the torrential cloudburst undermined and washed out the pavement, so that today Golden Canyon is a wonderful place for hikers only. This pattern of drought and torrent follows countless periods of flash floods, shattering rockslides, and a wetter era when the alluvial fan was preceded by an ancient shallow sea. This is a land in constant flux.

At stop 2 it is easy to see how the canyon was carved out of an old alluvial fan made up of volcanic rock that predates Death Valley's origin some 3 million years ago. Layers in the rock tell the tales of periodic floods over the eons. Just above, the canyon displays tilted bands of rock, where faulting caused huge blocks of the earth's crust to slide past one another. The Furnace Creek formation is the compilation over time of lakebed sediments dating back about 9 million years. The ripple marks of water lapping over the sandy lakebed hardened into stone as the climate warmed; the marks are evident on the tilted rock. Weathering and the effects of thermal water produced the splash of vivid colors seen today.

Mountain building to the west gradually produced a more arid climate, causing the lake to dry up. At the same time, the land was tilted by the widening and sinking of Death Valley and by the uplift of the Black Mountains. Dark lava from eruptions 3 to 5 million years ago slowed erosion, explaining why Manly Beacon juts so far above the surrounding badlands. These stark badlands rising above the canyon at mile 0.5 are the result of rapid runoff from storms on erodible, almost impermeable rocks.

Several narrow side canyons invite exploration on the way up Golden Canyon, particularly those opposite stop 2, and to the left and just above stops 6 and 7. The interpretive trail ends at stop 10, about 1 mile up the canyon at an elevation of 140 feet. For the short hike, this is your turnaround point.

Options

For a 0.8-mile round-trip hike to the base of Red Cathedral, continue up the broken pavement. Hike past the old parking area to a narrow notch at 320 feet, directly below the cathedral's looming presence. Red Cathedral was once part of an active alluvial fan, washed out from the Black Mountains to the south. The bright red color results from the weathering of iron to produce the rust of iron oxide. The cliff faces are made up of the more resistant red rock crowning softer yellow lake deposits.

Upon returning to stop 10 at mile 1.8, follow the signed trail to your left (east) up a steep gully well marked with trail posts. The trail climbs across badlands beneath the imposing sandstone jaw of Manly Beacon. At 2.3 miles you reach a high ridge saddle below Manly Beacon at 440 feet. Follow the markers down a side gully to a wash/trail junction at 2.6 miles. The left-hand wash leads eastward up to Zabriskie Point. The right-hand wash/trail descends west to Gower Gulch.

If you walk up the main wash, you quickly come to the artificial cut made in the rock wall to divert Furnace Creek through Gower Gulch. This cut has sped up erosion in the gulch. Note the gray color of the rocks washed in from Furnace Creek, which lie on the bottom of the drainage in contrast to the reds and yellows of the badlands. Gower Gulch is largely the result of human construction to protect Furnace Creek from serious flooding.

For a short side trip toward Zabriskie Point, turn left (south) at the junction and follow the markers for about 0.5 mile to excellent views of Zabriskie Point, the surrounding badlands, Death Valley, and the distant Panamint Range. Zabriskie Point is another 0.7 mile and 200 feet above, and is accessible by road from the other side. It does indeed provide one of the most magnificent views in all of Death Valley, but its proximity to a paved road may detract from the hiking experience on the Golden-Gower loop. Thus, the overlook below Zabriskie Point is recommended as the turnaround point for a scenic side trip. Zabriskie Point is a popular starting point for those hiking 3 miles downhill through Gower Gulch, then across to the mouth of Golden Canyon.

Back at the trail junction at mile 3.6, there is no marker post to point the way toward Gower Gulch. Simply continue down the wash toward wide, gray Gower Gulch, which drops below mounds of golden badlands. At 3.9 miles a side wash intersects the main wash; continue downward to the right. Early-day miners in search of borax pocketed the walls of Gower Gulch with tunnels. These small openings are

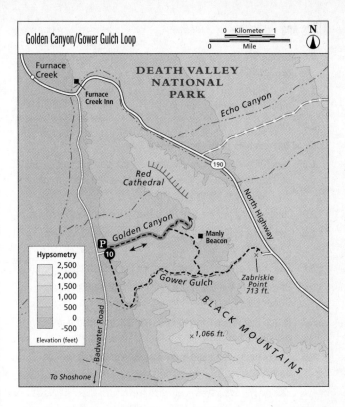

Golden Canyon/Gower Gulch Loop

0 Kilometer 1

0 Mile 1

N

Furnace
Creek

DEATH VALLEY
NATIONAL
PARK

Furnace
Creek Inn

Echo Canyon

190

Red
Cathedral

Golden Canyon

Manly
Beacon

North Highway

Hypsometry

2,500
2,000
1,500
1,000
500
0
-500

Elevation (feet)

Gower Gulch

Zabriskie
Point
713 ft.

BLACK

Badwater Road

×1,066 ft.

MOUNTAINS

To Shoshone

unsecured and potentially dangerous. A mile down, the wide
gravel wash bends sharply left, narrowing dramatically with
the bedding and faulting of red and green rock. The canyon
floor then quickly drops 40 feet to below sea level.

At 5.2 miles the wash meets a 30-foot dry fall. A good
user trail curves around the rock face to the right. From
here the faint but easy-to-follow trail heads north 1.3 miles
along the base of the mountains, paralleling the highway
back to the Golden Canyon parking area, completing the
loop and side trips.

Miles and Directions

0.0 Depart from the Golden Canyon trailhead (160 feet below sea level).

1.0 Reach the end of the interpretive trail at stop 10. Turn around and retrace your steps.

2.0 Arrive back at the trailhead.

Optional intermediate points or complete loop

1.8 Reach the intersection with the 0.8-mile side trip to the base of Red Cathedral. Backtrack to stop 10 and the beginning of the trail toward Manly Beacon.

2.3 The high point of the trail (440 feet) is below Manly Beacon.

2.6 Arrive at a trail/wash junction between Gower Gulch and Zabriskie Point.

3.1 Reach the overlook below Zabriskie Point (500 feet).

3.6 Backtrack to the trail/wash junction; begin to hike down Gower Gulch.

5.2 Reach the 30-foot dry fall in Gower Gulch; take the trail around to the right.

6.5 Complete the loop and arrive back at the Golden Canyon trailhead.

11 Harmony Borax Works

This short hike on a loop trail leads to a historic nineteenth-century industrial site on the valley floor. There are interpretive signs along the trail. The endless borax flats are an overwhelming sight.

Distance: 1-mile loop
Hiking time: Less than 1 hour
Elevation change: Minimal
Difficulty: Easy
Trail surface: Asphalt walkway to Harmony Borax Works (wheelchair accessible); sandy trail to overlook and to salt flats
Best season: October through March

Fees and permits: National Park entrance fee (see DVNP website)
Maps: NPS Death Valley Visitors Map; Trails Illustrated Death Valley National Park Map; USGS 1:24,000 topo maps Furnace Creek West-CA and Furnace Creek-CA

Finding the trailhead: The trailhead for the Harmony Borax Works Trail is 1.3 miles north of the park visitor center at Furnace Creek on CA 190. The 0.2-mile road on the left (west) is signed. The asphalt walkway leads west of the parking area. An optional 5-mile round-trip hike to the salt flats begins at the far side of Harmony Borax Works, heading west from the loop trail. GPS: N36 28.812' / W116 52.407'

The Hike

This desolate site was the scene of frenzied activity from 1883 to 1888—not in quest of gold, like so much mining activity, but of borax. Used in ceramics and glass as well as soap and detergent, borax was readily available here in Death Valley. Borax prices were mercurial due to soaring supply and moderate demand in the nineteenth century, so the industry was plagued by sharp boom and bust cycles. Here at the Harmony Works, the years of prosperity were typically brief.

Chinese laborers hauled the borate sludge in from the flats on sledges to the processing plant, the remains of which are the focal point of the hike. There, the borate was boiled down and hauled 165 miles across the desert to Mojave by the famed twenty-mule teams. One of the wagons that made this journey stands below the borax plant. Although the works were in operation only from October to June, working conditions for man and beast were harsh. For more information about the history of mining in Death Valley, visit the Borax Museum (free admission) at Furnace Creek Ranch.

Although this is a short hike, be sure to bring plenty of water. It's a dehydrating experience.

Options

A 0.5-mile side hike to a low hilltop overlook gives you an excellent vista of the central valley floor. From here, it is easy to imagine the usual workday in operation at the Harmony Works. To the east of the hilltop is an area that appears to have been a dump for Furnace Creek. A rusty antique car rests on the hillside, surrounded by desert.

You can also reach Harmony Borax Works by way of a 1-mile-long bicycle path along CA 190 from Furnace Creek.

A longer optional hike into the flats—of about 5 miles round-trip—confirms the arduous nature of the work on the valley floor. An unsigned but well-trod path leads west from the end of the paved loop. It travels by a damp slough where groundwater percolates to the surface, causing borate crystals to form. Farther out on the flats, mounds of borax mud

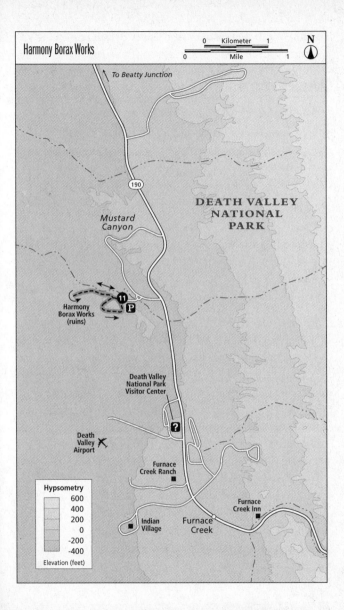

Harmony Borax Works

0   Kilometer   1

0   Mile   1

N

↑ To Beatty Junction

190

Mustard
Canyon

DEATH VALLEY
NATIONAL
PARK

11 P

Harmony
Borax Works
(ruins)

Death Valley
National Park
Visitor Center

?

Death
Valley
Airport

Furnace
Creek Ranch

Furnace
Creek Inn

Indian
Village

Furnace
Creek

Hypsometry

600
400
200
0
-200
-400

Elevation (feet)

remain where the laborers made piles to validate the works' mining claim more than a hundred years ago.

Miles and Directions

0.0 Depart from the Harmony Borax Works trailhead.

0.2 A trail leads south from the asphalt path to the hilltop.

0.5 Reach the outer end of loop; a user trail extends out into the borax flats.

1.0 Arrive back at the parking area.

12 Salt Creek

A nature trail on a boardwalk along Salt Creek features unique vegetation and wildlife, such as pickleweed, salt grass, and endemic Salt Creek pupfish found only here. There is an optional hike on the east ridge.

Distance: 0.5-mile lollipop loop
Hiking time: Less than 1 hour
Elevation change: Minimal
Difficulty: Easy
Trail surface: Boardwalk; user trail for longer option
Best season: February through April
Fees and permits: National Park entrance fee (see DVNP website)

Maps: NPS Death Valley Visitors Map; Trails Illustrated Death Valley National Park Map; USGS 1:24,000 topo map Beatty Junction-CA
Trailhead facilities: The signed parking area with vault toilets, picnic tables, and a signed interpretive trail is at the end of the road.

Finding the trailhead: From the park visitor center in Furnace Creek, drive north on CA 190 for 13.8 miles and turn left (southwest) on the signed road to the Salt Creek Interpretive Trail. GPS: N36 35.444' / W116 59.442'

The Hike

Salt Creek Interpretive Trail is a fully accessible, lollipop-shaped boardwalk hike, with trailside signs providing interpretive information. The extended hike continues 2 miles up Salt Creek to the Salt Creek wetlands. There is a beach-like quality to the short hike, not only due to the boardwalk designed to protect this delicate habitat, but also due to the aroma of salt water, and the salt grass and pickleweed growing in dense clumps on the sandy stream banks.

The Salt Creek pupfish, endemic to Death Valley, are the stars of this hike. It's hard to believe these tiny relicts of the Ice Age can continue living in the hottest, driest place in the United States. In the spring hundreds of pupfish swim in the riffles and pools of the creek. The fish are visible only February through May, with peak activity during March and early April. In other seasons they are either dormant (winter), or the stream is reduced to isolated pools (summer and fall).

The boardwalk runs alongside the creek and then crosses it in several spots—the first bridge is at 0.1 mile—so it provides an excellent vantage point to watch the pupfish in the clear shallow water or the deep pools. Pupfish are fast, are small (not much longer than an inch), and enjoy zipping up and down the shallow riffles to bunch up in schools in the deeper terminal pools. As prehistoric Lake Manly dried up and grew saltier, these little fish were able to adapt to the new salty environment. Slimy green and brown algae, caddisflies, beetles, and water boatmen flourish here too, providing an adequate diet for the pupfish.

The walk out along Salt Creek is a startling change from the usual Death Valley desert floor hike. The sound of the merry running water in the winter and spring, with the flourishing growth of salt grasses, suggests a stroll on the beach. All that is missing are the seagulls. With the interpretive signs along the trail, you can enjoy the fish and birds as well as learn about the dynamic changes of the desert habitat and the ability of some species to adapt to the harsh conditions.

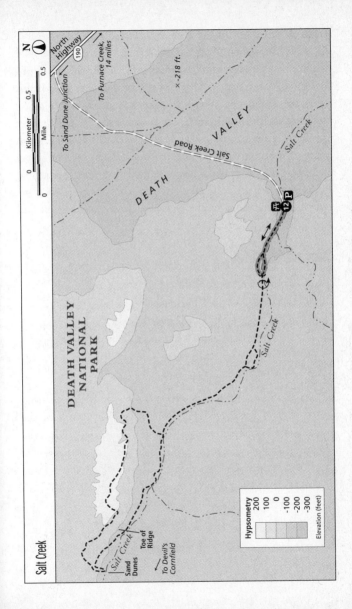

Salt Creek

DEATH VALLEY NATIONAL PARK

DEATH VALLEY

Salt Creek Road

To Sand Dune Junction

To Furnace Creek, 14 miles

North Highway 190

×-218 ft.

Salt Creek

Salt Creek

Salt Creek

Sand Dunes

Toe of Ridge

To Devil's Cornfield

N

Kilometer
0   0.5

Mile
0   0.5

Hypsometry	
200	
100	
0	
-100	
-200	
-300	
Elevation (feet)	

12 P

Option

To leave the developed boardwalk trail, take the user trail from the far (west) end of the loop at 0.2 mile where it drops down steps at the eastern side of the bridge. The path heads north along the east side of Salt Creek. You can amble along the path, out and back, for as far as you want. Along the way you'll see more pupfish and a variety of birds. This is a good place to spot a great blue heron. Another option is to climb the ridge directly east of the extended hike and hike about 0.5 mile to a high point that rises 150 feet above Salt Creek, offering nice views up the drainage. These routes will add about 4 miles to the trip.

Miles and Directions

0.0 Begin at the boardwalk west of the parking area.

0.1 Go straight to the first bridge for proper number sequence.

0.2 The user trail by the bridge at the end of the loop leads up Salt Creek; continue on the boardwalk to return to the parking area.

0.5 Arrive back at the parking area.

13 Mesquite Flat Sand Dunes

These sand dunes cover more than 14 square miles, the largest area of any of the seven major sand dunes in the park. They are also the most easily accessible from a road and very scenic with a scattered mantle of mesquite trees and a surprising array of nocturnal wildlife. As such, they are the most popular and heavily visited sand dunes in Death Valley National Park. This hike takes you to a more remote corner of the dunes where you'll see a lot more tracks of wildlife than of humans. To see the most animal tracks before they are obscured by wind and shifting sand, get there during the dramatic light of early morning.

Distance: 2 to 4 miles, depending on how large a circle through the dunes you make
Hiking time: 1 to 3 hours
Elevation change: Minimal
Difficulty: Easy
Trail surface: Two-track trail, loose to compacted sand
Best season: November to April
Fees and permits: Park entrance fee (see DVNP website)
Maps: NPS Death Valley Visitors Map; Trails Illustrated Death Valley National Park Map; USGS 1:24,000 topo map Stovepipe Wells NE-CA
Special considerations: During the hotter months ground temperatures can exceed 180 degrees F. Carry ample water even during short hikes, at least twice what you think you'll need. Do not attempt this hike during the heat of the summer or anytime when temperatures exceed 100 degrees F. Once in the dunes it is easy to become disoriented and lose track of where you started from, especially if you're dehydrated. From the trailhead carefully mark a key point that you can remember. You'll then be able to visually navigate back toward it to the trailhead if you get turned around.

Finding the trailhead: From Stovepipe Wells drive 7.5 miles east on CA 190 to the junction with Scotty's Castle Road. Continue left (north) on Scotty's Castle Road 2.9 miles and turn left (west) onto the historic Stovepipe Wells Road. If coming from the north on Scotty's Castle Road, the turnoff is 32.7 miles south of Grapevine. Follow this dirt road 0.8 mile to the road closure at the wilderness boundary. Here you'll find a large parking area, a monument to Old Stovepipe Wells, and the original Stovepipe Well. GPS: N36 39.543' / W117 04.764'

The Hike

This leisurely sandy stroll takes you to dunes that are lower than the 100-foot-high dunes near the expanded parking area 2.5 miles east of Stovepipe Wells. The payoff is a far less crowded opportunity to experience the Mesquite Flat Sand Dunes. The interesting Old Stovepipe Wells monument at the parking area is in itself worth the short drive from Scotty's Castle Road. The monument sits next to the original wellhead of the only waterhole in the Death Valley sand dunes, at the junction of two Indian trails. When sand began covering up the wellhead, a length of stovepipe was inserted, hence its distinctive name.

Begin by hiking southward along a two-track trail that was once known as the Sand Dunes Picnic Area Road. This old closed two-track has been converted to an excellent hiking trail. The two-track nature of the trail is fading in places, thanks to it being closed to vehicular traffic at the wilderness boundary near the trailhead. The boundary is marked by a large wooden Wilderness Restoration sign. As you walk along the trail, you'll parallel the east-central edge of the extensive Mesquite Flat Sand Dunes with a grand view straight ahead of Tucki Mountain, a massive mound that rises nearly 5,000 feet above the valley floor.

The Mesquite Sand Dunes are formed by north winds that carry sand down Death Valley until backing up against the buttress of Tucki Mountain, causing the sand to amass at its foot. Southerly winds have formed a vast eddy on the leeward side of Tucki, adding yet more sand. The dunes are ever shifting but are trapped in place.

After about 1 mile the trail bends to the right to meet the dunes. This is a good place to leave the trail and venture southwesterly into the dunes. In early spring during a good flower year, you'll see an abundance of wildflowers, especially desert gold and evening primrose. Dense clusters of bright green mesquite crown the tops of small dunes. In canyon bottoms 20-foot-tall mesquite are short trees, but here, in the harsh environment of the dunes, they are only a tall shrub. Yellow catkins cover the plant during late spring, which become long brown bean pods by early fall. These sweet pods are favored by an amazing array of desert denizens. To survive on an average of less than 2 inches of annual precipitation, and in some years no rain at all, mesquite can send a taproot more than 150 feet deep.

One of the great joys of dune trekking is looking for and trying to identify a myriad of animal tracks. The mostly hard-packed sand provides an ideal palette for recording the artistry of prints, at least for a few hours until they are erased by windblown sand. You'll find evidence of kangaroo rats, lizards, beetles, and several kinds of snakes, including sidewinder rattlesnakes with their distinctive sidewinding imprint.

For your cross-country dune hike, imagine a giant half circle that begins with a southwesterly sweep that gradually angles west, then north, then northeast back to the trail that you started the hike on. Follow it northward to the parking area. Along the way you'll see several types of dunes, with the most obvious being barchan (crescent-shaped) dunes with arms trailing downwind. You may also find transverse dunes along linear ridges at right angles to the prevailing wind and perhaps even a localized star dune or two. The highest dune is actually called Star Dune. The graceful curves and varied colors, ripples, and shadows of the dunes will pull you in different directions, which is all the more reason to wander without any particular destination in mind.

If you've marked a point on the southern Grapevine Mountains to navigate toward, you'll have no trouble intersecting the trail just south of the parking area. Good, recognizable features to mark include the Death Valley Buttes and aptly named Corkscew Peak.

Option

You can start the hike from the south where the two-track trail intersects CA 190, about 1.1 miles southwest of the junction of CA 190 and Scotty's Castle Road. GPS: N36 37.714' / W117 03.113'

The trail angles to the northwest. After about 1.5 miles you'll reach the same edge of the dunes described above from the north. Turn left (west) and wander off-trail into the dunes, making a broad circle in the opposite direction described above. After circling west to south to southeast, you'll eventually intersect the trail you started on. Turn right (south) to get back to where you parked alongside CA 190.

Miles and Directions

0.0 Depart from the Stovepipe Wells (northern) parking area.

1.0 The trail bends right to meet the dunes. This is the turn-around point for the shorter hike.

2.0 Arrive back at the trailhead.

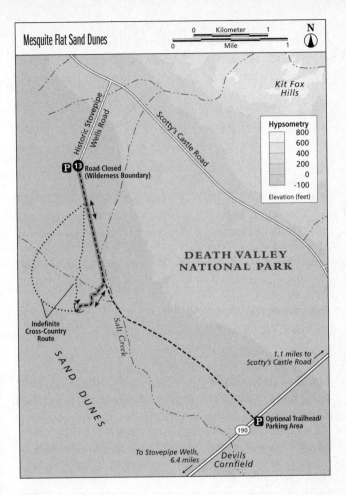

Mesquite Flat Sand Dunes

Kit Fox Hills

Historic Stovepipe Wells Road

Scotty's Castle Road

P ⑬ Road Closed
(Wilderness Boundary)

Hypsometry

	800
	600
	400
	200
	0
	-100

Elevation (feet)

**DEATH VALLEY
NATIONAL PARK**

Indefinite
Cross-Country
Route

Salt Creek

1.1 miles to
Scotty's Castle Road

S A N D D U N E S

P Optional Trailhead/
Parking Area
190

To Stovepipe Wells,
6.4 miles

Devils
Cornfield

Option

1.0 Wander into the dunes and make a circle so as to intersect the trail after hiking 1 to 3 miles.

2.0-4.0 After meeting the trailhead, walk north the short distance to the parking area.

14 Monarch Canyon/Mine

This out-and-back hike leads you down a rocky canyon in the Funeral Mountains to an 80-foot dry fall, a well-preserved historic stamp mill, and a desert spring with bird-watching opportunities.

Distance: 1.8 miles out and back from the end of Monarch Mine Road; 3 miles out and back from Chloride City Road
Hiking time: 2 to 3 hours
Elevation change: 310 feet from Monarch Mine Road; 540 feet from Chloride City Road
Difficulty: Easy
Trail surface: Four-wheel-drive road, rocky trail, clear wash

Best season: October through April
Fees and permits: National Park entrance fee (see DVNP website)
Maps: NPS Death Valley Visitors Map; Trails Illustrated Death Valley National Park Map; USGS 1:24,000 topo map Chloride City-CA

Finding the trailhead: From Daylight Pass Road 3.4 miles east of Hell's Gate Junction in Boundary Canyon and 15.8 miles southwest of Beatty, Nevada, look for a road to the south marked only with a small sign recommending four-wheel drive. Carefully driven high-clearance two-wheel-drive vehicles can negotiate this road for 2.2 miles to the bottom of upper Monarch Canyon. High-clearance four-wheel drive is required for vehicular travel beyond this point to Chloride City. The rough Monarch Mine Road takes off south from this point. This road junction can serve as the trailhead for the hike down Monarch Canyon. However, you can shorten the hike by 1.2 miles if you drive down Monarch Mine Road to a point just above the dry fall; four-wheel drive is required. GPS: N36 44.216' / W116 54.736'

The Hike

You can start at the unsigned junction between the rough Chloride City Road and four-wheel-drive Monarch Mine Road (3 miles round-trip to Monarch Spring) or at the end of the Monarch Mine Road (1.8 miles round-trip). From the Chloride City Road junction, the trip starts out in rounded, low-lying hills. The four-wheel-drive road descends south-westerly, entering a rocky canyon after 0.3 mile.

At 0.6 mile the road ends above a striking 80-foot dry fall. A major side canyon enters from the left, bounded by high cliffs marked by folded multicolored bands of rock. Continue left around the fall on the old mining trail. After another 0.1 mile the trail drops to the wash, which is covered with horsetails and Mormon tea. This is favored habitat for quail and other birds. The base of the dry fall is definitely worth visiting, so turn right and walk 0.1 mile up to the precipice. In addition to the main wide fall, another smaller but equally high fall guards the canyon bowl to the left. The canyon walls are distinguished by shelf rock catch basins, overhangs, and contorted layers of colorful, twisted rock.

As you proceed down the sandy canyon wash, an eroded mining trail crosses to the right and then drops back to the canyon floor at 1.0 mile. Cairns are in place for the return trip. At 1.2 miles you reach the wood and cement ruins of the Monarch Mine stamp mill on the left (southeast). The ore chute to the mill extends up an almost vertical rock face. For more information about the history of mining in Death Valley, visit the Borax Museum (free admission) at Furnace Creek Ranch.

To further experience the rugged grandeur of Monarch Canyon, continue down the wash another 0.3 mile to the

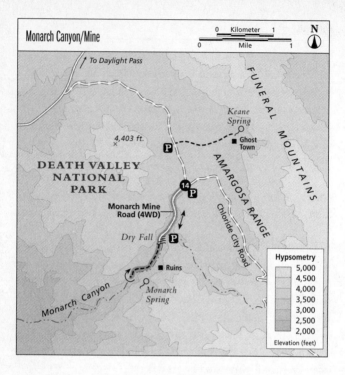

Monarch Canyon/Mine

0 Kilometer 1
0 Mile 1

N

DEATH VALLEY NATIONAL PARK

To Daylight Pass

FUNERAL MOUNTAINS

Keane Spring

Ghost Town

4,403 ft.

P

14 P

AMARGOSA RANGE

Monarch Mine Road (4WD)

Chloride City Road

Dry Fall

P

Ruins

Monarch Spring

Monarch Canyon

Hypsometry
5,000
4,500
4,000
3,500
3,000
2,500
2,000
Elevation (feet)

brushy bottom just below Monarch Spring. Here, the canyon bends sharply to the right and narrows. Hiking below the spring would be difficult due to dense vegetation and loose, rocky side slopes. Retrace your route.

Note: A popular nearby hiking destination is the Keane Wonder Mine and Springs, located a few miles south of Monarch Canyon. At the time of this writing this entire area was closed to all visitor access due to mine safety hazards. The park is working to mine-safe Keane Wonder Mine and vicinity and anticipates reopening it to the public. Check with the Furnace Creek Visitor Center (760-786-3200) for the current status.

Miles and Directions

0.0 Depart from the trailhead at the junction of the Chloride City Road and Monarch Mine Road in upper Monarch Canyon.

0.6 Reach Monarch Mine Road's end and an 80-foot dry fall.

0.7 The mining trail drops to the bottom of the canyon wash.

0.8 Walk up the wash to the base of the dry fall.

1.2 Reach the Monarch Mine stamp mill ruins.

1.5 Arrive at Monarch Spring.

3.0 Arrive back at the trailhead on Chloride City Road by the same route.

15 Titus Canyon Narrows

Titus Canyon contains the most popular backcountry road in the park. The rough four-wheel-drive road is also popular as a hiking route. And little wonder, for it has almost all of what Death Valley is famous for—rugged mountains, colorful rock formations, hanging gardens of rare plants, majestic cliffs, arched caverns, a ghost town, petroglyphs, wildlife, and a deep narrow canyon.

Distance: 4.2 miles out and back; 13 miles out and back to Klare Spring optional
Difficulty: Easy; strenuous for longer hike due to distance and elevation gain
Elevation change: 650 feet on shorter route; 2,100 feet to Klare Spring
Trail surface: Rocky, high-clearance four-wheel-drive road

Best season: October through April
Fees and permits: National Park entrance fee (see DVNP website)
Maps: NPS Death Valley Visitors Map; Trails Illustrated Death Valley National Park Map; USGS 1:24,000 topo map Fall Canyon-CA
Trailhead facilities: A vault toilet and information kiosk are located at the parking area.

Finding the trailhead: The two-way road to the mouth of Titus Canyon is 17.3 miles north of the junction of Scotty's Canyon Road and CA 190, and 17.9 miles south of the Grapevine Entrance Station on Scotty's Castle Road. Take the signed dirt road east for 2.7 miles up the alluvial fan to the Titus Canyon mouth, where there is a parking area and a vault toilet. The parking area is about 36 miles north of Furnace Creek. Titus Canyon Road is one-way from the east, beginning at the canyon mouth. Embark on this hike early in the morning to reduce the chance of meeting vehicles. GPS: N36 49.330' / W117 10.421'

The Hike

Titus Canyon is the longest and one of the grandest canyons in Death Valley. Morris Titus was a prospector who disappeared in the canyon in 1906 while searching for help after running out of water. Titus Canyon Road was built in 1926 to serve the town of Leadville, an investor scam that became a ghost town the following year. This 26-mile one-way unpaved road is accessible only by high-clearance four-wheel-drive vehicles.

Visiting majestic Titus Canyon by vehicle may not be the most satisfactory way to enjoy its scenery. By driving the 2.7-mile two-way portion at the western end of Titus Canyon Road, you can park and walk through the dramatic narrows of the canyon. Seeing it on foot increases the majesty of the canyon.

Titus Canyon is narrow enough to almost be a slot canyon, immediately narrow at its mouth. From the brightness of the desert floor you plunge into the canyon's cool shadows. Cliffs tower hundreds of feet above. Breezes rush down through the funnel of the canyon. The display of cliffs continues without intermission for 2 miles as you hike up the primitive canyon road. The variety of colors and textures on the canyon walls is immense and ever changing. The limestone layers are twisted and folded; fault lines run at all angles. In addition to the power of the earth's surface to rise and fall and shift, the power of water is visible throughout the narrows. The water-smoothed walls indicate the level of flooding. The curves of the canyon's path reveal the erosive power of the swift floods as they roar down the tight opening with their load of scouring boulders. Flash floods are a real danger in Titus; often the road is closed for days after a

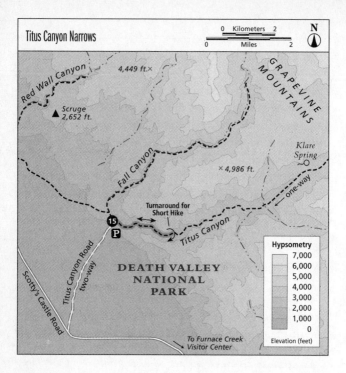

Titus Canyon Narrows

0 Kilometers 2

0 Miles 2

N

Red Wall Canyon

4,449 ft.×

GRAPEVINE MOUNTAINS

▲ Scruge 2,652 ft.

Fall Canyon

Klare Spring

× 4,986 ft.

one-way

Turnaround for Short Hike

15

P

Titus Canyon

Titus Canyon Road two-way

DEATH VALLEY NATIONAL PARK

Scotty's Castle Road

Hypsometry

7,000
6,000
5,000
4,000
3,000
2,000
1,000
0

Elevation (feet)

To Furnace Creek Visitor Center

storm in the area. Check for conditions at the Furnace Creek Visitor Center (760-786-3200) before your outing.

The 2.1-mile hike through the narrows is overpowering. Like walking down the nave of a European cathedral, hiking up (and later down) Titus is a soaring experience, but also an immensely humbling one. The Titus Canyon Fault, which created the canyon, slices through the heart of the Grapevine Mountains, laying their innards bare for both the geologist and layman to enjoy. With the road as a walking surface, you can totally devote your attention to the details of this mountain cross-section, a rare occasion when hiking in Death Valley.

Option

For a longer hike continue up the road another 4.4 miles to Klare Spring. The canyon floor is considerably broader, although quite steep, after you leave the narrows at 2.1 miles, but the towering peaks of the Grapevines still provide a spectacular backdrop for the canyon hike. The spring is on the north side of the road at 6.5 miles. Springs are critical habitat for bighorn sheep, which gather nearby in hot summer months. Some marred petroglyphs are above the spring, a reminder that it is both unlawful and boorish to harm such artifacts. Return the way you came, enjoying your downhill trip, thereby completing a long 13-mile hike.

Miles and Directions

0.0 Follow the four-wheel-drive road east into Titus Canyon.

2.1 The narrow canyon opens into a broader valley. This is the turnaround for the short hike.

4.2 Arrive back at the trailhead.

Option

2.1 From the valley continue on the optional hike to Klare Spring.

6.5 Klare Spring is on north side of the road; petroglyphs are east of the spring. This is the turnaround for the long hike.

13.0 Arrive back at the trailhead.

West and North of Death Valley

16 **Wildrose Trail**

The Wildrose Trail takes you to a high Panamint saddle, and from there to the summit, from which the highest and lowest land in the lower forty-eight states can be seen. This is a cool alternative to the heat of lower elevations. Highlights include historic charcoal kilns, a rugged canyon, and scenic views of Death Valley.

Distance: 3.6 miles out and back to saddle; 8.4 miles out and back to peak

Hiking time: 2 to 3 hours; 5 to 6 hours if climbing the peak

Elevation change: 740 feet to saddle; 2,100 feet to the summit of Wildrose Peak

Difficulty: Moderate; strenuous if climbing to the summit

Trail surface: Clear dirt path

Best season: September through mid-November; March through June (depending on snow levels)

Fees and permits: National Park entrance fee (see DVNP website)

Maps: NPS Death Valley Visitors Map; Trails Illustrated Death Valley National Park Map; USGS 1:24,000 topo maps Telescope Peak-CA, plus Wildrose Peak-CA for those climbing the peak

Trailhead facilities: There are vault toilets at the Wildrose Charcoal Kilns parking area.

Finding the trailhead: From CA 190 at Emigrant Junction, drive south on Emigrant Canyon Road for 20.9 miles to Wildrose Junction; continue east on Mahogany Flat Road (paved for 4.5 miles) and drive 7.1 miles to the Wildrose Charcoal Kilns parking area. In winter this road may be impassable; check with park authorities at Furnace Creek Visitor Center (760-786-3200) for weather and road conditions. The signed trailhead to Wildrose Peak is about 36 miles south of Stovepipe Wells. It begins at the north end of the kilns. GPS: N36 14.766' / W117 4.528'

The Hike

The Wildrose Trail is one of only two constructed trails in the park. It travels through classic pinyon pine–juniper forest to a high saddle, then zigzags to the broad, open summit of this central peak in the Panamint Range.

In spite of the impressive elevation gain to the peak, Wildrose Trail begins modestly. From the kilns at the trailhead, the trail charges 50 yards uphill to the northwest, gaining 60 feet, but then follows the contour of the hillside for the next mile. This section is a gentle warm-up for those climbing the peak. Along the route, rock outcroppings extend to the west, hovering over Wildrose Canyon below. This is stereotypic mountain lion country.

Climbing only slightly, the trail joins an old logging trail coming up from the canyon. Numerous pine stumps are a reminder of the logging done here more than a century ago to supply the charcoal kilns during their brief use in the 1870s.

At the head of the canyon at 0.9 mile, the trail begins its climb. After about 1.2 miles the trail bends north and steepens sharply, gaining more than 600 feet in less than a mile. Rising to the first saddle at 1.8 miles, you have a magnificent view through the evergreens of Death Valley below. Unless you are climbing the peak, this is a good turnaround point.

Option

Wildrose Peak provides panoramic views of Death Valley and the surrounding mountain ranges. This broad, open summit in the central Panamint Range is reached via an 8.4-mile round-trip hike, with a vertical gain of 2,100 feet. Telescope Peak and Wildrose Peak are served by maintained trails and are the only hikes recommended during summer because of extreme heat at lower elevations. Parts of the Wildrose Trail may be icy and snow covered from November into April.

The trail climbs around three small rises before emerging on a ridge above the saddle below the peak. Here, at 3.1 miles and 8,230 feet, you can pause and view the 90-mile length of Death Valley. From the saddle a mile of switchbacks leads to the summit. The trail snakes north, then south, then north, and so on, up the 834-foot climb. The changing direction enables you to enjoy a variety of vistas as you ascend the mountain, particularly as you near the windswept summit, which is clear of major vegetation. The meadow-like mountaintop is nearly always windy; appropriate clothing is a requirement, as are binoculars to enjoy the sweeping 360-degree view. Summer hikers will appreciate bug dope to combat flies and gnats. Don't be discouraged by the false summit on the south peak at 4.1 miles. Just beyond view and only another 0.1-mile lies the true summit at 9,064 feet.

A small rock wall on the peak was designed to give some protection from the wind. Or you can drop just a few feet down on the leeward side of the mountain to enjoy your stay and write a note for the peak registry. From Wildrose you can see the vast area of mining activity in the north end of the Panamint Range. Just to the northeast, in the canyon below, there is a massive mining camp. Farther along Emigrant Canyon Road, mining roads crisscross the mountainsides. Rogers (with a microwave station) and Telescope Peaks loom above to the south. To the west is the mighty wall of the Sierras. To the east, across the valley, rise the Funeral and Black Mountains.

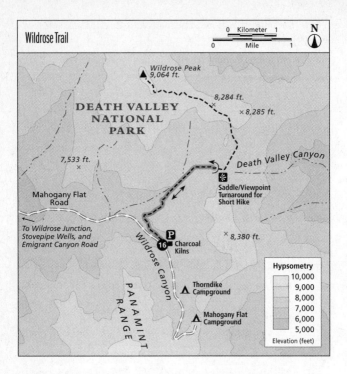

The hike back down the mountain allows you to relax and focus on a new view of the scenery. Death Valley Canyon, extending eastward below the high saddle, is just one of the dramatic sights you may notice on the downward trip. Although this is a heavily used trail, its bending pathway preserves a feeling of solitude for the hiker.

Miles and Directions

0.0   Depart from the trailhead on the north side of the kilns.

0.9   Reach the head of Wildrose Canyon.

1.2   The trail bends and steepens.

1.8 Climb the saddle; views of Death Valley and Badwater open to the east.

3.6 Arrive back at the trailhead..

Optional climb to Wildrose Peak

1.8 Continue north on the trail.

2.9 Reach a second saddle with more panoramas.

4.1 Arrive on the south peak, the false summit.

4.2 On the north peak, the genuine summit, you will find a register in an ammo box.

8.4 Arrive back at the trailhead.

17   Nemo Canyon

The Nemo Canyon hike takes you on a gentle downhill traverse through open desert along a wide graveled wash, bounded by low ridges and multicolored badlands, providing a pleasing contrast to nearby mountain climbs. Several short, narrow side canyons branch out along the way.

Distance: 4-mile shuttle
Hiking time: 3 to 4 hours
Elevation change: 1,450-foot descent
Difficulty: Moderate due to distance
Trail surface: Cross-country without a trail; open graveled wash
Best season: October to May
Fees and permits: National Park entrance fee (see DVNP website)
Maps: NPS Death Valley Visitors Map; Trails Illustrated Death Valley National Park Map; USGS 1:24,000 topo map Emigrant Pass-CA
Special considerations: In the past the Wildrose Canyon Road has been closed due to washout. Check the road status at the Furnace Creek Visitor Center (760-786-3200). If the road is closed, Nemo Canyon can be enjoyed as an out-and-back hike of 4 to 8 miles round-trip.

Finding the trailhead: From Wildrose Junction (0.2 mile west of the Wildrose Campground), drive 2.2 miles north on the paved Emigrant Canyon Road. Turn left (northwest) onto an unsigned gravel road that takes off from the paved road as it veers right (northeast). Drive 0.7 mile to the end of the road at a paved T next to a gravel pit. A USGS benchmark is adjacent to this spot, which is the trailhead and jumping-off point for the hike. The parking area is about 27 miles south of Stovepipe Wells. GPS: N36 17.547' / W117 11.594'

The end point is the broad mouth of Nemo Canyon on Wildrose Canyon Road, which is located down the canyon 3 miles southwest of Wildrose Junction and 1 mile southwest of the picnic area.

The Hike

This down-canyon traverse begins in open desert country dotted with creosote brush and Mormon tea. Nemo Canyon drops moderately to the southwest. To avoid walking toward the sun and into a stiff afternoon wind, make this a morning excursion if possible.

The canyon is wide open with low-lying hills and ridges—a pleasing contrast to nearby mountain climbs. Soon, a few scattered yucca begin to appear. At first the wash is braided and graveled but it becomes better defined, with a sandy bottom, after about 1 mile. At 1.5 miles the valley narrows a bit. After another 0.2 mile red rhyolite bluffs rise on the left (south) side. Around the corner the valley opens in a semicircle, with several side canyons entering from the right (north). The white saline seep of Mud Spring is also to the right (north) at 2.0 miles.

At 2.2 miles 100-foot-high cliffs rise on the left (south) as the canyon narrows slightly. After another 0.2 mile the wash parallels brightly colored badlands—red, white, black, gray, pink, and tan—with steep bluffs rising several hundred feet on the left. At 2.4 miles a huge valley enters from the right (north). At 3.2 miles the canyon is marked by brown, deeply eroded conglomerate cliffs and spires. Large granite boulders appear, resting precariously atop spires of brown conglomerate. At times loose gravel impedes walking, but the steady downhill grade helps.

At 3.8 miles the canyon opens to the wide Wildrose Valley. In just another 0.2 mile, Nemo Canyon meets the rough Wildrose Canyon Road, thereby completing this point-to-point downhill traverse.

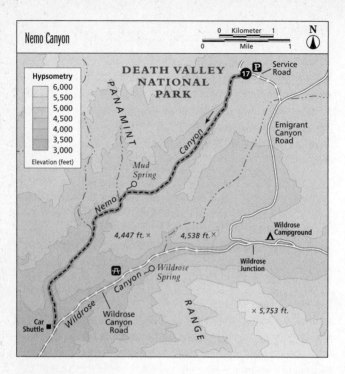

Miles and Directions

0.0 Start from the trailhead in Nemo Canyon wash.

2.0 Reach Mud Spring.

4.0 Finish the hike at Wildrose Canyon Road.

18 Aguereberry Point and Eureka Mine

Two short hikes feature spectacular views from high on the edge of the Panamint Range overlooking Death Valley. Eureka Mine provides an excellent view of a gold miner's life in the last century.

Aguereberry Point

Distance: 0.4 mile out and back to the overlook; 1.6 miles out and back to the promontory

Hiking time: About 20 minutes for short route; 1 to 2 hours for longer hike

Elevation change: Overlook minimal; 420 feet gain/loss for promontory

Difficulty: Easy for short route; moderate for longer hike

Trail surface: Dirt, gravel, some rocks

Fees and permits: National Park entrance fee (see DVNP website)

Best season: October to April; always check weather reports

Maps: NPS Death Valley Visitors Map; Trails Illustrated Death Valley National Park Map; USGS 1:24,000 topo map Wildrose Peak-CA

Special considerations: At 6,433 feet, with no protection, this is not a place you want to be in stormy or high wind conditions.

Trailhead facilities: None, but there is an informational sign at the parking area.

Finding the trailhead: From Stovepipe Wells, drive southwest on CA 190 for 8 miles. Turn left (south) on Emigrant Canyon Road. Drive south 11.6 miles and turn left on Aguereberry Point Road. This is a slow, very twisty gravel road. At 2.3 miles you will pass the Harrisburg site and the remnants of Aguereberry's Eureka Mine, which you'll want to visit on the way down. The road winds through shrubby foothills to arrive abruptly at a jaw-dropping overlook at a T intersection 6.2 miles from Emigrant Pass Road. Turn left and continue 0.2 miles to the parking area at the summit. GPS: N36 211.474' / W117 02.880'

The Hikes

The Overlook: At the parking area you have arrived at a spectacular spot in the Panamint Range, looking out at Death Valley. An information sign at the trailhead provides the history of the Basque miner who developed the Eureka mine and created this road to share the view. After your drive through the rolling foothills, this perch is breathtaking.

Follow the suggestion on the sign and take the user trail around the north side of the ridge. It goes out to a point beyond the jutting rocks. Although there are no dangerous places on the hike, this is not a hike for anyone with vertigo or fear of heights. At the overlook there are convenient sitting rocks where you can enjoy the peaceful view, if there is no strong wind.

The naked geology of the Panamints and Death Valley is laid out before you. Massive alluvial fans pour out of the Panamint canyons and ravines onto the valley floor. The great faulted mountains cut the sloping strata as they dive into the valley below. Tetracoccus Ridge, right in front of you, blocks your view of the Furnace Creek settlement, but all of Death Valley's grandeur is right there at your feet.

This is a mountaintop experience without the climbing, as well as the shortest hike with the biggest payoff.

Miles and Directions

0.0 Start at the parking area.

0.2 End of path.

0.4 Arrive back at the parking area.

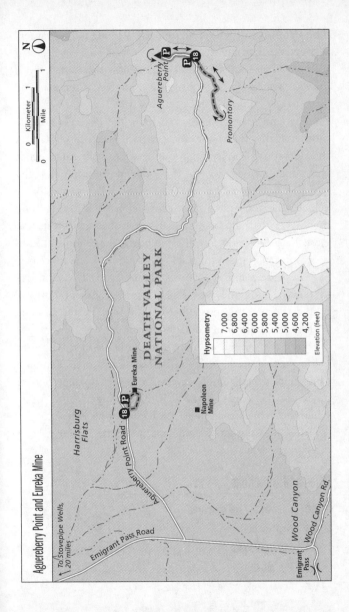

Aguereberry Point and Eureka Mine

Harrisburg Flats

To Stovepipe Wells, 20 miles

Emigrant Pass Road

Emigrant Pass

Wood Canyon

Wood Canyon Rd.

Aguereberry Point Road

Eureka Mine

Napoleon Mine

DEATH VALLEY NATIONAL PARK

Aguereberry Point

Promontory

Hypsometry

7,000
6,800
6,400
6,000
5,800
5,400
5,000
4,600
4,200

Elevation (feet)

N

0   Kilometer   1

0   Mile   1

The Promontory Hike: Drive back 0.2 mile to the T intersection and park there. The hike starts out on a former Jeep track, heading southwest. The track is now barricaded and is being rehabilitated to its original condition. After the long drive to the Point, this is a lively leg stretcher.

The faint gravel two-track fades in the first saddle, demonstrating that the restoration program is effective. Stay on the ridgetop 0.4 mile to a mound, where your route bends westward. Stay always on the ridgeline, heading for the nameless promontory to the west. Now out of sight of your vehicle, the route continues across another soft ridge and then up to the hilltop another 0.4 mile ahead. No Jeep trail exists here. Do-si-do through the brittle bush, going around rock outcroppings, to the 6,433-foot point on the topo map.

There are plentiful coyote droppings as well as old traces of burros along the way. The clusters of rodent burrows mimic the miners' adits wherever the dirt is soft enough, with gigantic slag heaps outside their holes.

From the summit an incredible mining road is visible far below to the south, winding in Trail Canyon to a mining camp tucked in a remote ravine. In the far distance pinyon pines dot the slopes of the Panamint Range to the south, while the striped strata dive into Badwater far below.

After enjoying the magnificent view, retrace your steps to the parking area.

Miles and Directions

0.0 Start at the parking area.

0.3 First saddle.

0.4 Top of mound.

0.8 Top of hill.

1.6 Arrive back at the parking area.

Eureka Mine

Distance: 1 mile loop
Hiking time: 1 to 2 hours
Difficulty: Moderate, with steep pitches
Trail surface: Miner pathways, crumbly gravel
Fees and permits: National Park entrance fee (see DVNP website)
Best Season: October to April
Maps: NPS Death Valley Visitor Map; Trails Illustrated Death Valley National Park Map; USGS 1:24,000 topo map Wildrose Peak-CA
Special considerations: Use extreme caution around mining sites. The park service has fenced off adits and shafts, but these industrial sites remain danger-ous, with unanticipated hazards. Keep a watchful eye on your companions.

Finding the trailhead: From Stovepipe Wells, drive 8 miles south-west on CA 190 to turn left on Emigrant Pass Road. Drive south 11.6 miles to turn left on Aguereberry Point Road. Drive 2.8 miles to the Eureka Mine turnoff on the right. Follow the graded two-track 0.2 mile to the turnaround and parking area next to Providence Ridge. GPS: N36 21.743' / W117 06.421'

If coming from Aguereberry Point, go back down the road 3.4 miles to the turnoff to the mine on the left. You can see the ruins of the mill on the slopes of Providence Ridge as you approach the site. Drive 0.2 mile to the turnaround and the parking area.

The Hike

The Eureka mine site is an interesting outing on many levels. Geology, as always, is intriguing, especially when pursuing gold. Here the human history provides another great tale. Pete Aguereberry worked this mine from 1905 to 1945, first as a partner with Shorty Harris, and then on his own. Providence Ridge, an unassuming rise sitting apart from the massive Panamints, is a surprising location for Pete's pot of gold, but it is estimated that he did relatively well here in his four decades of work.

The information sign at the parking area provides the mining history as well as information on the endangered Townsend big-eared bat, which uses the mine as a winter home. The adits have bat gates welded in place. These have horizontal bars so the bats can come and go, but humans can't.

From the parking area wander up the ridge along any of the numerous pathways created by Pete. The ridge is pockmarked with adits and shafts. The park service has fenced off many of the dangerous shafts that dive downward into darkness, but watch your step. Holes are everywhere and footing is sketchy on the crumbly gravel.

Around the ridge, rusted mine litter is everywhere. As a visitor you may admire these artifacts, but remove nothing. Track, pipes, barrels, stoves, a truck, a 1940s car—it's all slowly rusting away.

Following the pathway west along the valley floor below the ridge, you come upon Aguereberry's camp. Here Shorty and Pete lived modestly, although their accommodations were superior to those in the now nonexistent tent city of Harrisburg, which spread out to the east of the ridge in the 1910s. Hundreds of optimists used to live there.

Some of Pete's buildings are still standing. Again, be careful when investigating these historical structures. A park service sign explains the history of the enterprise. For more information about the history of mining in Death Valley, visit the Borax Museum (free admission) at Furnace Creek Ranch.

From the camp head up the ridge on the pathway behind Pete's house. This was his route to and from work for forty years. Dropping back to the parking area near the Cashier Mill, you can admire the work involved in a successful gold mine. This was not an easy way to make a living

Miles and Directions

0.0   Start at the parking area.

0.3   Top of Providence Ridge.

0.6   Aguereberry Camp.

0.9   Cashier Mill.

1.0   Arrive back at the parking area.

19 Darwin Falls

Highlights of Darwin Falls include bird-watching along a year-round desert stream, with a forked waterfall in a densely vegetated canyon gorge. The delightful moist microclimate of the falls is tucked away in a secluded canyon.

Distance: 1.8 miles out and back
Hiking time: 1 to 2 hours
Elevation change: 170 feet
Difficulty: Easy
Trail surface: Dirt path and sandy wash
Best season: October through June
Fees and permits: National Park entrance fee (see DVNP website)
Maps: NPS Death Valley Visitors Map; Trails Illustrated Death Valley National Park Map; USGS 1:24,000 topo map Darwin-CA
Trailhead facilities: There is a signed trailhead parking area with a bulletin board at the end of the rough dirt road.
Special considerations: This is a day-use-only area. There is no swimming or bathing allowed at the spring since this is the water supply for nearby Panamint Springs.

Finding the trailhead: From Panamint Springs, 29.6 miles southwest of Stovepipe Wells on CA 190, drive west for 1.1 miles to the signed Darwin Falls Road on the left. Turn left (southwest) on the dirt road, and drive 2.6 miles to the signed side road on the right (south) for Darwin Falls. You will notice a pipeline running along the road. The road is rough but passable for a standard passenger vehicle to the signed trailhead parking area. GPS: N36 19.686' / W117 30.870'

The Hike

Darwin Falls is nestled at the western edge of the expansion area of Death Valley National Park, adjacent to the 8,600-acre Darwin Falls Wilderness Area managed by the Bureau of Land Management immediately west of the park.

Darwin Stream is the only permanent water in this west-central region of the park. Flowing from the China Garden Spring, Darwin supplies the Panamint Springs Resort with water via a pipeline visible on both the drive and the hike to the falls. This year-round water source sustains dense willow and cottonwood thickets in the valley and canyon, as well as a thriving bird population. Swifts and red-tailed hawks soar overhead, and are among the more than eighty bird species that have been seen here. Brazen chuckwallas stare at intruders from their rocky lairs.

This hike is a radical change from the usual Death Valley outing. From the higher level of the parking area, you can see a streak of greenery and a glistening brook leading up the gently sloping valley floor. Drop to the narrow stream and step across it to pick up the well-worn sandy path on the east side of the canyon. Around the bend the canyon narrows and the foliage becomes denser. Here is a blast of greenery. The Darwin Mountains, composed of black rhyolite, tower above the bright green grass, the willow saplings, the horsetails, and cattails.

Visitors to Darwin Falls have created a plethora of likely pathways through the jungle. Some of these pathways are suitable for agile youngsters, whereas others are less challenging. Seasonal rains can cause flooding in the canyon, erasing some of the pathways. Along the right side of the stream valley is the access track for the town's maintenance of the

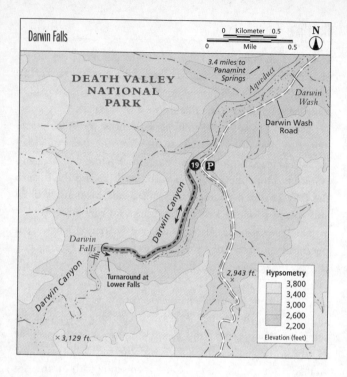

0   Kilometer   0.5

0   Mile   0.5

N

DEATH VALLEY NATIONAL PARK

3.4 miles to Panamint Springs

Aqueduct

Darwin Wash

Darwin Wash Road

19 P

Darwin Canyon

Darwin Falls

Turnaround at Lower Falls

Darwin Canyon

2,943 ft. ×

× 3,129 ft.

Hypsometry
3,800
3,400
3,000
2,600
2,200
Elevation (feet)

aqueduct. This track can become muddy. Narrow paths to avoid the mud wind through the thickets. Beware of the boulders, which are very slippery when wet.

There are many bends in the narrow canyon. With the steep canyon walls, as well as the willow and cottonwood thickets, this shady Garden of Eden offers an excellent outing on a hot, sunny day!

At 0.9 mile you reach the falls, after hearing them in the distance. Double falls cascade over a 25-foot drop-off, surrounded by large old cottonwoods. Sword ferns, watercress, and cattails flourish in the pool below. This is the turnaround point. Hiking above the waterfall is both difficult and dangerous. The park service has had to rescue numerous visitors who were stranded on cliffs trying to reach the upper falls.

Emerging from Darwin Canyon is like an Alice-in-Wonderland experience. After you've been surrounded by humidity and greenery, the beige desert looks one-dimensional. The valley below the canyon is a striking transition zone, with the soft greenery of the stream ecosystem juxtaposed against the jagged dark rhyolite cliffs of the mountains to the south. The hike to Darwin Falls is a carnival of sensory perceptions. The smells, sounds, feel, and sights of this watery world make this an exceptional experience.

Miles and Directions

0.0 Pick up the trail that follows the stream up the narrow valley floor.

0.9 Reach the lower falls.

1.8 Arrive back at the trailhead by the same route.

20 Mosaic Canyon

Mosaic Canyon is a showcase of geologic wonder, so hiking into the canyon is like walking into a museum. Patterned walls of multicolored rock and water-sculpted formations await you in this picturesque northern Tucki Mountain canyon.

Distance: 2.8 miles out and back to the lower dry fall; 4 miles out and back to the upper dry fall

Hiking time: 2 to 3 hours

Elevation change: 700 feet to lower dry fall; 1,000 feet to upper dry fall

Difficulty: Easy to lower dry fall; moderate to upper dry fall

Trail surface: Dirt path with rock, then open canyon floor

Best season: Late October into April

Fees and permits: National Park entrance fee (see DVNP website)

Maps: NPS Death Valley Visitors Map; Trails Illustrated Death Valley National Park Map; USGS 1:24,000 topo map Stovepipe Wells-CA

Trailhead facilities: There is a vault toilet and an information board at the Mosaic Canyon parking area.

Finding the trailhead: Go 0.1 mile southwest of Stovepipe Wells Village on CA 190, then head south (left) on the signed Mosaic Canyon road, which is rough but passable with two-wheel drive. After 2.3 miles the road ends at the large Mosaic Canyon parking area. The trail takes off immediately (south). GPS: N36 34.253' / W117 8.652'

The Hike

The fault in Tucki Mountain that produced Mosaic Canyon consists of mosaic breccia and smooth Noonday formation dolomite, formed in a seabed 750 to 900 million years ago. After being pressurized and baked at more than 1,000 degrees, then eroded, the resulting rock has startling contrasts of both texture and color.

Mosaic Canyon drains more than 4 square miles of the Tucki Range, so avoid it, like all canyons, in flash flood conditions. Rushing water, carrying its load of scouring boulders, has created smooth, marbleized waterways out of the otherwise lumpy breccia. Silky surfaces on the canyon floor gradually change to rugged lumps higher up its walls, reflecting the varying depths of floodwaters.

Like other canyons in Tucki Mountain, Mosaic Canyon is alternately wide and narrow. The wider spots are more numerous and broad enough almost to qualify as inner valleys. Often hikers arrive at these open areas and turn back, figuring the canyon excitement has ended. With plenty of water and a broad-brimmed hat, you can continue exploring the depths of Mosaic Canyon. If it's a hot day, be aware that this is not a deep, shady canyon like those in the Grapevine and Funeral Mountains. This canyon offers little protection from the sun.

The first 0.2 mile of canyon features the polished marble surfaces that have made Mosaic Canyon a favorite destination of Death Valley visitors. After that the canyon opens to a wide, colorful amphitheater, swinging eastward to a broad valley with a 40-foot butte standing in the center. User trails go in all directions, converging at the end of the valley where the canyon narrows again. To the right of the butte, a deep wash will eventually become a new branch of Mosaic Canyon.

At 1.0 mile a small pile of boulders blocks a narrow spot. A well-traveled path to the left (east) provides an easy

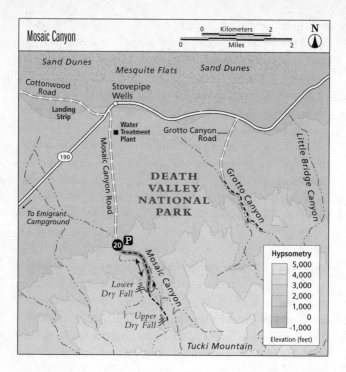

Mosaic Canyon

0 Kilometers 2
0 Miles 2

N

Sand Dunes

Mesquite Flats   Sand Dunes

Cottonwood
Road

Stovepipe
Wells

Landing
Strip

Water
Treatment
Plant

Grotto Canyon
Road

Little Bridge Canyon

190

DEATH
VALLEY
NATIONAL
PARK

Grotto Canyon

Mosaic Canyon Road

To Emigrant
Campground

20 P

Mosaic Canyon

Lower
Dry Fall

Upper
Dry Fall

Tucki Mountain

Hypsometry

5,000
4,000
3,000
2,000
1,000
0
-1,000

Elevation (feet)

detour. After another wide spot, the canyon narrows again, where an abrupt 40-foot dry fall blocks your passage at 1.4 miles. The hike back down the canyon provides new views of Death Valley and the Cottonwood Mountains in the distance. Sliding down the short water chutes on the return to the trailhead increases the marbleized beauty of these breccia formations; generations of hikers have added to water's erosive force in creating these smooth rocks.

You can sometimes see bighorn sheep above Mosaic Canyon, so keep a watchful eye out for these reclusive desert denizens.

Option

It is possible to get around the dry fall on a well-traveled, marked trail. Drop 50 yards back from the dry fall to the trail on the sloping canyon wall to the south. This path takes you to the upper region of Mosaic Canyon, where another 0.5 mile and 300 feet of elevation gain through marbleized chutes and narrows await you. A steep marble funnel, 50 feet high, halts the hike at about 2 miles. It's a striking spot, with eroding, fragmented Tucki Mountain rising above the silky smooth waterslide.

Miles and Directions

0.0 The trail begins in a wash from the parking area behind the information sign.

0.2 Enter the wide-open canyon.

1.4 A 40-foot dry fall blocks the canyon.

2.8 Arrive back at the trailhead.

Option

1.4 Fifty yards before the lower dry fall, take the side trail to the upper dry fall.

2.0 The upper dry fall blocks further passage. Turn around and retrace your steps to the trailhead.

4.0 Arrive back at the trailhead.

21 Grotto Canyon

This out-and-back Tucki Mountain canyon hike winds through water-carved grottos and narrows of polished rock to a high dry fall.

Distance: 4 miles out and back
Hiking time: 2 to 3 hours
Elevation change: 800 feet
Difficulty: Easy
Trail surface: Sandy rocky wash, then open canyon floor
Best season: Late October through April

Fees and permits: National Park entrance fee (see DVNP website)
Maps: NPS Death Valley Visitors Map: Trails Illustrated Death Valley National Park Map; USGS 1:24,000 topo map Grotto Canyon-CA

Finding the trailhead: The Grotto Canyon access road heads south from CA 190, 2.4 miles east of Stovepipe Wells Village. The road is signed for Grotto Canyon and four-wheel-drive vehicles. The road ends for most vehicles after 1.1 miles south of CA 190, at which point the road changes to soft gravel above the wash. The road/trail continues up the wash to the canyon. Park next to a turnaround at the end of the dirt road before reaching the wilderness boundary sign. GPS near the canyon mouth: N36 35.30' / W117 6.70'N36 35.486'/W117 6.633'

The Hike

With careful driving, a two-wheel-drive vehicle can negotiate the road to the wash of the Grotto Canyon hike. For the additional mile to the canyon entrance, the wash's soft gravel requires high clearance and four-wheel drive. A wilderness/no vehicles sign marks the end of the road. Conditions in this

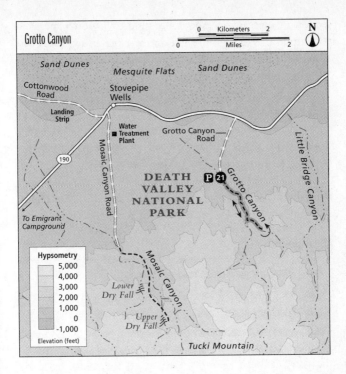

Grotto Canyon

	0	Kilometers	2
	0	Miles	2

N

Sand Dunes

Mesquite Flats

Sand Dunes

Cottonwood Road

Stovepipe Wells

Landing Strip

Water Treatment Plant

Grotto Canyon Road

Little Bridge Canyon

190

DEATH VALLEY NATIONAL PARK

Mosaic Canyon Road

P 21

Grotto Canyon

To Emigrant Campground

Hypsometry
- 5,000
- 4,000
- 3,000
- 2,000
- 1,000
- 0
- -1,000

Elevation (feet)

Mosaic Canyon

Lower Dry Fall

Upper Dry Fall

Tucki Mountain

canyon change with each flood. At times the gravel is deep and the dry falls easy to scale, but often floods have scoured away the gravel, making exploration more of a challenge.

Like the other Tucki Mountain canyons, Grotto Canyon is very broad—up to 200 yards wide in many areas. Deeply eroded canyon walls stand like medieval castle ramparts, with short serpentine pathways in their lower reaches. The narrows at 1.8 miles bring welcome shade after the journey up the graveled canyon bottom. A pair of ravens nesting in the aerie alcove above the grotto may provide suitable visual and sound effects for the hiker approaching this almost cave-like section of the canyon. About 0.1 mile back down the canyon, a trail marked with cairns on the eastern side leads you around this barrier to the canyon above. Another dry fall at 2.0 miles will block your travels.

Even with its proximity to Stovepipe Wells, Grotto Canyon is not heavily visited. The adventuresome hiker can enjoy desert exploration and solitude without a lengthy drive on dirt roads. The intense silence above Mesquite Flat envelops you between cries of the ravens.

As you hike back to the road, the dunes stretch out below, framed by the Cottonwood and Grapevine Mountains. Grotto Canyon is a desert wonder of a smaller dimension.

Miles and Directions

0.0 Follow the gravel Jeep road up the wash.

0.9 The canyon narrows.

1.8 Reach the first dry fall.

2.0 Arrive at the second dry fall.

4.0 Follow the canyon and arrive back at the trailhead.

22 The Grandstand

The Grandstand is a high mound of dark rock contrasting dramatically within the gleaming white Racetrack Playa. A mountainous backdrop, intense isolation, and outstanding scenic views await the visitor.

Distance: 1 mile out and back
Hiking time: Less than 1 hour
Elevation change: Minimal
Difficulty: Easy
Trail surface: Smooth sand
Best season: October through April

Fees and permits: National Park entrance fee (see DVNP website)
Maps: NPS Death Valley Visitors Map; Trails Illustrated Death Valley National Park Map; USGS 1:24,000 topo map Ubehebe Peak-CA

Finding the trailhead: From the junction of Scotty's Castle Road and Ubehebe Crater Road in the northeastern corner of the park, head northwest on the paved Ubehebe Crater Road. The pavement ends after 5.3 miles at the turnoff to Ubehebe Crater. Continue south on the washboard, dirt Racetrack Valley Road for 19.7 miles to Teakettle Junction. Take the right-hand turn for Racetrack Valley Road and drive another 5.7 miles to the Grandstand parking area, which is opposite the "grandstand" of gray rocks in the dry lakebed east of the road. The parking area with an interpretive sign is adjacent to the dirt Racetrack Valley Road and is about 82 road miles northwest of Furnace Creek. GPS: N36 41.594' / W117 35.561'

The Hike

The Grandstand is about 0.5 mile directly east of the parking area. It consists of a large, 70-foot-high mound of gray rocks rising in stark contrast to the surrounding white flatness of

The Grandstand

0 Kilometer 1
0 Mile 1

N

DEATH VALLEY
NATIONAL PARK

The Grandstand
3,713 ft.

RACETRACK VALLEY

Hypsometry
6,000
5,600
5,200
4,800
4,400
4,000
3,600
3,200
Elevation (feet)

Ubehebe Peak
5,678 ft.

THE
RACETRACK
PLAYA

× 5,230 ft.

× 3,708 ft.

LAST CHANCE RANGE

Racetrack Valley Road

5,335 ft. ×

"Moving
Rocks"

× 5,428 ft.

× 3,963 ft.

the Racetrack Playa, a dry lakebed. For added perspective, walk around the Grandstand, then scramble up some of the large boulders. The Grandstand can be easily climbed 40 to 50 feet above the playa. Don't expect to see the famous "moving rocks" here, as they are found a couple of miles to the south. The Grandstand provides a superb perspective of formidable 5,678-foot-high Ubehebe Peak, rising 2,000 feet 1.5 miles to the west.

Options

Drive south from the Grandstand another 2 miles. Look for a short user trail heading east across the southern end of the 3-square-mile pancake-flat Racetrack Playa. This is where you will find the best view of the strange trails of the mysterious moving rocks. The secret of these mobile rocks was partially solved when researchers actually saw them moving in December 2014. The stones, some of which weigh hundreds of pounds, move slowly by wind-driven ice that forms on the playa and then breaks up under very rare conditions.

Miles and Directions

0.0 Head east from the Grandstand trailhead.

0.5 Reach the Grandstand.

1.0 Walk west across the playa and arrive back at the trailhead.

23 Ubehebe Lead Mine/Corridor Canyon

This exploration of a historic early-twentieth-century mine site with a tram will appeal to history and mining buffs. The longer leg in Corridor Canyon will enchant those who appreciate scenic vistas of desert cliffs and mountains.

Distance: 1 mile out and back to mine; 5 to 10 miles out and back in canyon

Hiking time: 1 to 2 hours to mine; 4 to 5 hours for the canyon, depending on the turn-around point

Elevation change: 380 feet on short hike; 1,000 feet plus or minus depending on turnaround for the longer hike

Difficulty: Moderate for both hikes due to steep slope to mine and distance in canyon

Trail surface: Dirt path to mine; clear wash in canyon

Best season: Late October through March

Fees and permits: National Park entrance fee (see DVNP website)

Maps: NPS Death Valley Visitors Map; Trails Illustrated Death Valley National Park Map; USGS 1:24,000 topo maps Ubehebe Peak-CA and Teakettle Junction-CA

Finding the trailhead: From Grapevine Junction take Ubehebe Crater Road northwest for 5.5 miles to the end of the pavement and the sign for Racetrack Valley Road. Turn right (southwest) onto Racetrack Valley Road. Four-wheel drive is recommended, but under normal weather conditions is unnecessary. Racetrack Valley Road is severely washboarded but contains no other obstacles as far as the Racetrack. Go south on Racetrack Valley Road for 19.6 miles to Teakettle Junction. Bear right (southwest), and continue for 2.2 miles to the right (west) turn to Ubehebe Lead Mine Road (signed). The dirt road leads 0.7 mile to a parking area at the mine site, which is near the end of the dirt road. The parking area is about 79 miles northwest of Furnace Creek. GPS: N36 44.712' / W117 34.902'

The Hike

Ubehebe Mine has a lengthy history, beginning in 1875 when copper ore was found here. The copper mine was not fully developed until early in the twentieth century, but the profitable ore was soon depleted. Lead mining began at the site in 1908 and continued until 1928. Ubehebe Mine had another renaissance in the 1940s as a zinc mine. Mining activity came to an end in 1951. For more information about the history of mining in Death Valley, visit the Borax Museum (free admission) at Furnace Creek Ranch.

After all this mining it is not surprising to find a plethora of mining artifacts in the valley and in the hills above. A miner's house has fallen down; its door and windows ajar, stripped of its plumbing (the range lies outside), it is a remnant of its midcentury inhabitants. Remember that it may be unwise to enter deserted buildings due to hantavirus from deer mice.

In the wash above there are other traces of the crude dwellings of miners. Stacked stone walls are still in place. The men worked inside rock walls by day and slept in them at night. Rusty debris and small, level tent sites are scattered about. A squeaky bedspring (burned and rusted) lies amid the creosote bushes. This is an appropriate place to pause and contemplate the bustle of activity and spirit of optimism that must have prevailed in this mining valley in its various heydays.

Below the housing area sits the ore chute, with rail tracks still leading from a mine opening. The area looks like it was deserted only a year ago. The sagging old tram cable still hangs from the tower atop the hill to the valley floor at 0.4 mile. Unsecured mine openings dot the hillside. Although the National Park Service has not posted its usual warning signs, do not get close to mines or shafts. The tram should also be given a wide berth.

The hike up the trail to the overlook at 0.5 mile gives you a magnificent aerial view of the mine encampment and the rolling hills of the Last Chance Range. Mine openings proliferate like rodent burrows. The rust-colored rock and earth in piles at each opening give the mining operations an eerily fresh appearance, as if the work here just stopped yesterday, instead of decades ago. Numerous wooden posts mark the mountainside along the trail to designate claims of long-gone prospectors. Crossing carefully beneath the hilltop tram tower, you arrive at trail's end and a view westward of winding Corridor Canyon.

A hike down Corridor Canyon is a nice addition to the Ubehebe Lead Mine hike. From the mine chute, drop generally westward down the wide and graveled wash to the head of Corridor Canyon. At 0.3 mile a tantalizing narrow stair-step chute of a canyon enters from the left (south), inviting exploration—although large boulders may prevent you from getting very far.

At about 1 mile impressive cliff walls soar high to the left (south), whereas the right (north) side is marked by folded rock layers altered by fault lines. Below, as the canyon turns left (west), are colorful bands of rock. The cliffs are pock-marked with caverns and other small openings, some of which serve as active dens for animals.

The canyon is unique in that it provides both a closed-in experience and vistas of distant cliffs, overshadowed by even higher cliff layers beyond, opening to expansive views

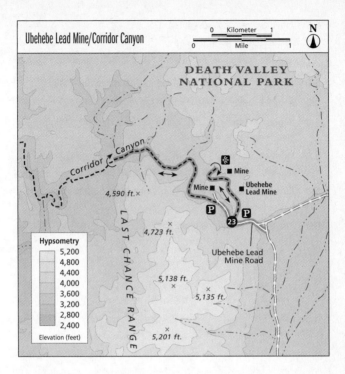

DEATH VALLEY
NATIONAL PARK

Corridor Canyon

■ Mine

Mine ■

■ Ubehebe
Lead Mine

4,590 ft.×

P

P

23

× 4,723 ft.

Ubehebe Lead
Mine Road

LAST CHANCE RANGE

5,138 ft.
×

× 5,135 ft.

× 5,201 ft.

Hypsometry

	5,200
	4,800
	4,400
	4,000
	3,600
	3,200
	2,800
	2,400

Elevation (feet)

of adjacent and faraway mountains. Hike another 1.5 miles
in the wide wash before turning around and retracing your
steps. For more of the same you can continue down the wash
for up to 2.5 additional miles, making for a pleasant day hike
of up to 10 miles out and back.

Miles and Directions

Mine hike

0.0 Back up the road from the miner's shack, on the north side
by the low stone wall, the trail leads up the hillside.

0.4 Pass a tram cable tower at the hilltop.

0.5 Arrive at the scenic overlook.

1.0 Arrive back at the trailhead.

Canyon hike

0.0 Just beyond the mine chute, head west down the wash.

0.3 A chute canyon enters from the left (south).

1.0 Reach the dramatic cliffs; continue down the canyon until you decide to turn around.

2.5 By this point you've seen what makes this canyon special, but you can continue for up to 2.5 more miles.

5.0 Anywhere along the route, turn around and retrace your steps to the trailhead.

10.0 Arrive back at the trailhead.

24 Ubehebe and Little Hebe Craters

These volcanic craters are a fascinating geology lesson on the forces that helped form Death Valley. A short loop hike around the large Ubehebe Crater and the several smaller ones allows you to witness the complex erosion patterns that have occurred since the craters' geologically recent birth.

Distance: 1.5-mile double loop
Hiking time: 1 to 2 hours
Elevation change: 320 feet
Difficulty: Easy; moderate to the bottom of the large crater
Trail surface: Volcanic cinder
Best season: Late October to April

Fees and permits: National Park entrance fee (see DVNP website)
Maps: NPS Death Valley Visitors Map; Trails Illustrated Death Valley National Park Map; USGS 1:24,000 topo map Ubehebe Crater-CA

Finding the trailhead: From the Grapevine Junction of Scotty's Castle Road and Ubehebe Crater Road, 45 miles north of Furnace Creek, take Ubehebe Crater Road northwest. Drive 5.7 miles to the parking area for the Ubehebe Crater/Little Hebe Crater trailhead. The signed parking area with interpretive signs is on the eastern side of the one-way loop of paved road at the end of Ubehebe Crater Road. GPS: N37 0.504' / W117 28.391'

The Hike

The volcanic region at the north end of the Cottonwood Mountains, near Scotty's Castle, is evidence of geologically recent cataclysmic events in Death Valley. The huge Ubehebe Crater was created around 300 years ago when magma heated groundwater and the pressure from the resulting steam blew the overlying rock away. This explosion covered 6 square miles of desert with volcanic debris 150 feet deep. Called a maar volcano by geologists, Ubehebe is a crater without a cone. The rim has been eroding ever since the explosion, gradually filling the crater with alluvial fans. Quite appropriately, the Shoshone Indians of Death Valley dubbed the crater "Basket in the Rock."

Little Hebe Crater, directly south, exploded even more recently, making it one of the newest geologic features of Death Valley. Little Hebe's rim is neat and well defined, exhibiting little of the erosion that has reduced Ubehebe's edge.

You can learn a lot about the craters by reading the information on the board and glancing at these monstrous holes in the earth. But there is no substitute for hiking all the way around this monumental display of volcanic power if you want to really appreciate the dimensions of the Ubehebe complex. Hold on to your hat, as this can be a very windy place.

The first quarter of the hike takes you along the rim of the main crater. The size of the hole is overpowering. It is almost a half mile from rim to rim. Alluvial fans have formed on the walls as the rains tear down the crater's edges.

In the vicinity of Ubehebe Crater, there are as many as twelve additional craters, all examples of more maar activity. You will see numerous craters in various stages of eroding deterioration. Little Hebe stands out as a jewel of a crater. Neat and trim, this volcanic chasm is only 200 yards across. The younger, fresher rim has barely begun to weather. Volcanic materials are very durable. Clearly visible on the walls of Little Hebe are the layers beneath the earth's surface. Especially noticeable is a thick layer of viscous lava that had oozed from the earth's interior prior to the explosion of Little Hebe.

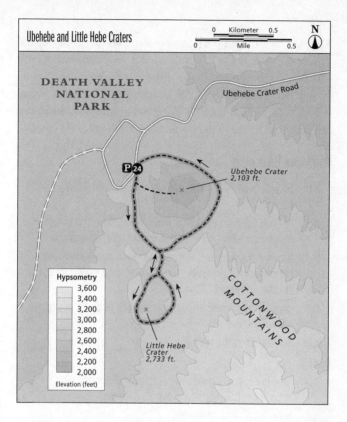

Ubehebe and Little Hebe Craters

0   Kilometer   0.5

0   Mile   0.5

N

DEATH VALLEY
NATIONAL
PARK

Ubehebe Crater Road

P 24

Ubehebe Crater
2,103 ft.

COTTONWOOD
MOUNTAINS

Hypsometry

3,600
3,400
3,200
3,000
2,800
2,600
2,400
2,200
2,000

Elevation (feet)

Little Hebe
Crater
2,733 ft.

After the tour around Little Hebe at 0.7 mile, continue your hike around the main crater, which seems even larger after visiting its younger neighbor. A well-defined trail leads around Ubehebe, ending at 1.5 miles. The power of nature to modify the terrain via volcanic action stands in sharp contrast to the more gradual erosive forces that are demonstrated elsewhere in Death Valley. The earth has not finished rearranging its surface here—the forces that created Ubehebe and Little Hebe are merely dormant, not dead.

Option

The 0.3-mile trail into the crater slopes downward from the rim at 1.3 miles. The volcanic cinder trail descends nearly 450 vertical feet to the floor of the crater. After major rainstorms the crater also features a small lake. Most of the time it is dry. The climb back to the parking area requires some exertion due to the skidding quality of the volcanic cinders.

Miles and Directions

0.0 Take the trail south from the information board at the parking area.

0.3 The trail climbs; bear left at the Y intersection. The trail to the right has eroded on both sides and may be hazardous.

0.4 Reach a maze of user trails on the small plateau between the craters; a sign directs you south to Little Hebe Crater. Follow the trail around Little Hebe.

0.7 Back at the intersection continue to hike around the large Ubehebe Crater.

1.5 Arrive back at the trailhead.

Option

1.3 Take the optional trail to the bottom of the crater, which adds about 0.6 mile to the overall distance.

2.1 Arrive back at the trailhead.

Day Hiker Checklist

Use the following checklist as you assemble your gear for day hiking in Death Valley National Park:

- ❏ sturdy, well-broken-in, light-to-medium-weight hiking boots
- ❏ broad-brimmed hat, with chin strap
- ❏ trekking poles
- ❏ long-sleeve shirt for sun protection
- ❏ long pants for protection against sun and brush
- ❏ water; two quarts to one gallon/day (depending on season), in sturdy screw-top plastic containers
- ❏ large-scale topographic map (quad) and GPS
- ❏ whistle, mirror, and matches (for emergency signals)
- ❏ flashlight or headlamp (in case your hike takes longer than you expect)
- ❏ sunblock and lip sunscreen
- ❏ insect repellent (in season)
- ❏ pocketknife
- ❏ small first-aid kit: tweezers, bandages, antiseptic, moleskin
- ❏ bee sting kit (over-the-counter antihistamine or prescription epinephrine) as needed for the season
- ❏ windbreaker (or rain gear in season)
- ❏ lunch or snack, with plastic bag for your trash
- ❏ toilet paper, with a plastic zipper bag to pack it out
- ❏ your FalconGuide

Optional gear

- ❏ camera
- ❏ binoculars
- ❏ bird and plant guidebooks
- ❏ notebook and pen/pencil

Help Us Keep This Guide Up to Date

Every effort has been made by the author and editors to make this guide as accurate and useful as possible. However, many things can change after a guide is published—trails are rerouted, regulations change, techniques evolve, facilities come under new management, etc.

We would appreciate hearing from you concerning your experiences with this guide and how you feel it could be improved and kept up to date. While we may not be able to respond to all comments and suggestions, we'll take them to heart, and we'll also make certain to share them with the authors. Please send your comments and suggestions to the following address:

> FalconGuides
> Reader Response/Editorial Department
> 246 Goose Lane
> Guilford, CT 06437

Or you may e-mail us at:

> editorial@falcon.com

Thanks for your input, and happy trails!

About the Authors

Polly and Bill Cunningham are partners in many outdoor adventures. They were owners of High Country Adventures, leading backpacking trips in the wilds of Montana and Alaska for nearly forty years until selling their guiding business in 2013. They now have more time to hike in favorite places, like Death Valley.

Polly and Bill coauthored FalconGuides' *Hiking California's Desert Parks, Wild Utah, Wild Montana, Hiking the Gila Wilderness, Hiking the Aldo Leopold Wilderness, Hiking Death Valley National Park,* and *Best Easy Day Hikes* guides to Anza-Borrego, Joshua Tree, and Death Valley. Writing about the vast and varied Death Valley National Park has been especially rewarding because long ago the authors both lived close to the California desert—Bill in Bakersfield and Polly in San Diego. They have enjoyed renewing their ties to California while exploring the state's desert regions. They want others to have as much fun exploring Death Valley as they did. They currently reside in Choteau, Montana.

AMERICAN HIKING SOCIETY

Because you hike.

We're with you every step of the way

American Hiking Society gives voice to the more than 75 million Americans who hike and is the only national organization that promotes and protects foot trails, the natural areas that surround them, and the hiking experience. Our work is inspiring and challenging, and is built on three pillars:

Volunteerism and Stewardship
We organize and coordinate nationally recognized programs—including Volunteer Vacations, National Trails Day ®, and the National Trails Fund—that help keep our trails open, safe, and enjoyable.

Policy and Advocacy
We work with Congress and federal agencies to ensure funding for trails, the preservation of natural areas, and the protection of the hiking experience.

Outreach and Education
We expand and support the national constituency of hikers through outreach and education as well as partnerships with other recreation and conservation organizations.

Join us in our efforts. Become an American Hiking Society member today!

American Hiking Society

1422 Fenwick Lane · Silver Spring, MD 20910 · (800) 972-8608
www.AmericanHiking.org · info@AmericanHiking.org